Embassies of Washington

EMBASSIES
of
WASHINGTON

CAROL M. HIGHSMITH AND TED LANDPHAIR

PHOTOGRAPHS BY
CAROL M. HIGHSMITH AND
DAVID PATTERSON

THE PRESERVATION PRESS

NATIONAL TRUST FOR
HISTORIC PRESERVATION

The Preservation Press
National Trust for Historic Preservation
1785 Massachusetts Avenue, Northwest
Washington, D.C. 20036

The National Trust for Historic Preservation is the only private, nonprofit organization chartered by Congress to encourage public participation in the preservation of sites, buildings, and objects significant in American history and culture. Support is provided by membership dues, endowment funds, contributions, and grants from federal agencies, including the U.S. Department of the Interior, under provisions of the National Historic Preservation Act of 1966. The opinions expressed here do not necessarily reflect the views or policies of the Interior Department. For information about membership in the National Trust, write to the Membership Office at the above address.

Printed in Singapore
96   95   94   93   92   5   4   3   2   1

Library of Congress Cataloging in Publication Data

Highsmith, Carol, 1946–
        Embassies of Washington / Carol M. Highsmith and Ted Landphair:
photographs by Carol M. Highsmith and David Patterson.
                p.   cm.
        Includes bibliographical references (p.   )
        1. Embassy buildings—Washington (D.C.)—History.
2. Washington (D.C.)—Buildings, structures, etc. I. Landphair,
Ted, 1942– . Patterson, David, 1960– . III. Title.
NA4443.W3H54 1992
725'.17—dc20 91-43141
ISBN 0-89133-170-0
ISBN 0-89133-190-5 (pbk.)

Cover:
Marble dancers on
the Y-shaped grand
staircase in the
Indonesian embassy
beckon to a promenade
gallery leading
to second-floor suites.
Page 2:
The gardens of the
British embassy
are the site of
one of Washington's
most coveted
diplomatic parties.
Page 3:
The residence of the
ambassador of Belgium
is a reproduction
of the Hôtel de
Charolais in Paris.

Contents

Acknowledgments

IT HAS BEEN A TREAT TO PRESENT, IN RICH PHOTO-graphic detail, the elegance and grandeur of the buildings that house the world's representatives in Washington. The diplomat's art has been employed with grace, not only by genial ambassadors and their hospitable spouses but also by the authors' associate, Dorothy M. Jones, whose charm opened many an embassy door and pried loose uncounted juicy details. The exquisite, and in some cases priceless, furnishings inside these buildings overwhelm the visitor, but extraordinary skill was required to arrange and light them in ways that evoke their splendor for readers of this book. Our photographic associates, Dave Hofeling and Neil Greentree, were masters at doing so.

Turning up the delicious stories of many of these properties proved equally challenging. You might think that an embassy staff would know all about the eccentric or ostentatious history of its building, but more often the here-today, gone-tomorrow diplomatic inhabitants haven't a clue. Wonderful studies by writer Hope Ridings Miller, the U.S. Commission of Fine Arts, and others have focused on some, but not many, of the embassies in detail.

When, for instance, the authors discovered that not one but two of the grand ambassadorial residences—of France and Portugal—had been built for the same man, a hitherto obscure figure named W. W. Lawrence, we were determined to learn more about him. That particular search took us to the Colorado mining territory, to Pittsburgh, where Lawrence and his father started a paint company, and to New York, where he and his wife hobnobbed in high society. It took some real spadework to uncover the reason this man of Pennsylvania and New York would build two luxurious Kalorama homes. For help in tracking down just that one elusive businessman, we are indebted to Princeton University archivist Ben Primer; to Harold Moldan, manager of the Sherwin-Williams Corporation's records division in Cleveland; to Walter Kidney, historian at the Pittsburgh History and Landmarks Foundation; and to Carl Miller at the mining museum in Leadville, Colorado.

Bruce Moffat at the Chicago Transit Commission gave us an enormous breakthrough in pinpointing another shadowy figure, Louis Owsley, who built the home that became the embassy of the Netherlands. John Hodges, archivist at the Navy Historical Center at the Washington Navy Yard, put us on the scent of Captain Thomas Moran, first owner of the residence now housing the Ecuadorian ambassador.

The wealth of broader research began with a thorough thumb-through of the marvelous programs of the Davis Memorial Goodwill Industries' embassy tours and galas, featuring Allison Brown's elegant sketches, which were cheerfully made available by Goodwill public relations manager Ruth P. Howard and explained by supervolunteer Mary Cavett Sims.

Deeper, rolled-up-sleeves-variety research was made pleasurable by a host of accommodating experts, including architect Francis Donald Lethbridge, who had been part of a survey of great Washington buildings; Joseph Mancias, Lee Feldman, Donald Jackson, and especially "institutional memory" George Oberlander of the National Capital Planning Commission, the agency in charge of managing the spread of chanceries; and Sue Kohler, historian for the U.S. Commission of Fine Arts, who helped produce four fact-filled volumes on Massachusetts Avenue and 16th Street houses.

Others who graciously opened treasure troves of information from their files included Orden Lantz, curator at the National Park Service's National Register of Historic Places; D.C. Public Library Washingtoniana Division librarians Matthew Gilmore, Mary Ternes, and Roxanna Dean; David Maloney of the D.C. Office of Historical Preservation; William Kay, a volunteer staff member, and curator Cheryl Miller, his supervisor, at the Historical Society of Washington library; George Caldwell at the Library of Congress; Carol Twombley, chief of the American Institute of Architects' library; Frank Aucella and Michael Sheehan at the National Trust for Historic Preservation's Wilson House; Howard Berger and Ann Hargrove of the Sheridan-Kalorama Citizens' Association; and Wayne Quin of the law firm Wilkes, Artis, Hedrick & Lane. Thanks, too, to Dick Pearson, Smith Wood, and Jackie Fleisher-Wood for being there when we needed them.

Finally, a special word of thanks to Hope Miller, the quintessential chronicler of the embassy scene, for her personal insights, guidance, and encouragement of our project. We trust that the final product slakes the curiosity of those who simply want to peer into the embassy world as well as those who crave richer information. Putting the package together has been a wonderful, collaborative experience.

Ted Landphair and Carol M. Highsmith

The photography was made possible by WASHINGTON FLYER magazine. Greenworks by Shane Floral, Inc., provided floral arrangements used in interior views of embassies.

Introduction

IT WAS AMERICANS, QUITE POSSIBLY PUTTING ON airs, who developed the notion that the great homes of foreign ambassadors should be called "embassies." Abroad, an embassy had traditionally been what Yankees call a "chancery," a utilitarian office for the paperwork business of state. But to an American visiting Washington to see the sights, an embassy has always meant that imposing, implicitly off-limits mansion where elegant dinners are spread; theme soirees thrown; dinner jackets, lavish gowns, and precious gems paraded; fine wines and finer cigars tasted; exotic tongues spoken; and fabulous furnishings from distant places savored. Even in times of international austerity this is not a fanciful picture. Just such an opulent world still swirls behind the wrought-iron gates and heavy oak doors of diplomatic Washington today. In *Embassies of Washington,* we pass through those gateways and open those doors to linger at some of these great homes — and several of the memorable chanceries as well.

Originally the word "embassy" had nothing to do with stone and mortar. An "ambassy" or "embassie" meant the envoy's affairs, or the retinue that carried them out. In *Love's Labour's Lost,* Shakespeare wrote, "Here comes in Embassie The French King's daughter." Sir William Temple in 1669 talked of "Lord Falconbridge, who is going on Embassy."

"Going on Embassy" was an idea grandly seized later that century by Peter the Great of Russia, who, after his ship almost foundered in the Baltic Sea, vowed to travel to the tomb of his patron saint in Rome to thank God for his deliverance. Ignoring the howls of his suspicious subjects and the insular Orthodox church, Peter had already opened Muscovy to foreign influence by cavorting in a "German quarter" of Moscow and employing Swiss officers like Francis Lefort to repel Tartar invaders. But when Peter launched the "Great Embassy," a journey through the western world to study customs, science, and shipbuilding, he set a never-equaled precedent for diplomatic junketing. Peter himself traveled incognito, as much as was possible for a man almost seven feet tall surrounded by a phalanx of boyars and bodyguards. He and his minions spent eighteen months abroad, but he never saw Rome.

It was to such free-floating delegations that the 17th-century English poet John Milton referred when he wrote of "Embassies from regions far remote," or that historian William Hickling Prescott, as late as 1843, had in mind when he spoke of "the embassy, consisting of two Aztec nobles, accompanied by the governor" in his treatise, *The Conquest of Mexico.* Not until the mid-19th century did an embassy come to mean a center for diplomatic intercourse. "It was a brilliant ball at the Palazzo of the Austrian embassy at Naples," reported the English novelist Edward Bulwer-Lytton in 1837.

The ancient Greek city-states had sent missions to one another and even developed the first rules of protocol — the "formula of international politeness." Key to protocol was a prohibition on accepting tribute (Virgil, three centuries later, picked up the theme: "I fear Greeks, even when they bring gifts"). Greek emissaries were distinguished elders in the Plato mold, not a professional cadre.

Roman law established the concept of diplomatic immunity,

Preceding pages: Villa Firenze, the Tudor residence of the Italian ambassador, sits on 22 lush uptown acres that had been the sixth most valuable piece of private property in Washington.

which was finally codified centuries later in 1961 as part of a Vienna treaty. The Romans accepted far more ambassadors than they deigned to send. Until the French perfected the art of diplomacy, Latin, spoken as well as written, was the accepted language. Today both English and French are de rigueur for the cultivated foreign representative—French since the early 19th century.

In the Middle Ages, warring knights were more worried about repelling barbarian assaults than defining the rules of court, and papal representatives handled most of the world's diplomatic chores. But by the late 15th century, Italian principalities had set up a network parallel to that of the Church, dedicated, in the fashion of Florentine Niccolò Machiavelli's later model, to international intelligence and intrigue.

With the emergence of Europe's great monarchies came the ceremonial pomp and rigid code of etiquette that defined the diplomat's calling. France's King Francis I dispatched the world's first permanent foreign representatives in the early 1500s, and the French were also the first to employ career diplomats and to institute competitive foreign-service exams. But all was not always civil in this civil service. In 1661, as the British prepared to greet a new emissary from Sweden, a battle royal (fought with swords, not conversation) ensued between the Spanish and the French as to whose coach should lead the welcoming procession. Spain prevailed, and the outraged Louis XIV retaliated by throwing the Spanish ambassador out of Paris.

England had quickly followed France in establishing a department of foreign affairs, going the French one better by dividing its secretariat into northern and southern departments, the better to serve the far-flung empire. Not surprisingly, the Prussians under Premier Otto von Bismarck introduced the idea of using foreign posts to drum up mercantile opportunities.·

At the Danish chancery, a self-portrait of the great uncle of the ambassador's wife sits on a lemonwood-inlaid oak secretary, carved in the 1700s in Schleswig-Holstein province.

International diplomacy, with its ostentatious trappings, soon attracted pretenders among the lesser states, whose own representatives scurried around the globe, prompting the English writer Aldous Huxley to remark, "Official dignity tends to increase in inverse ration to the importance of the country in which the office is held." Rules of diplomatic precedence were first codified at the congresses of Vienna in 1815 and Aix-la-Chapelle three years later. The rules still apply. In Catholic countries, papal nuncios generally represent the various diplomatic delegations when a collective voice is needed; in other countries, the dean

You might guess long and hard before correctly identifying this hacienda as the residence of the ambassador of Sweden. It was built for David Lawrence, the founder of U.S. NEWS & WORLD REPORT.

of the corps is the ambassador of longest standing. In Washington, that senior ambassador also gets the coveted DPL-1 license tag for his or her automobile. The 19th-century congresses also defined the pecking order for emissaries: ambassador (full title: ambassador extraordinary and plenipotentiary), legate or nuncio, followed by the envoy or minister, with chargés d'affaires left to long for career advancement.

Until the 18th century, a minister generally did not travel abroad with his wife; thereafter, diplomatic privileges began to be extended to her as well as to the ambassador's top-level entourage. Only envoys who were persona grata were to be accepted by the nations to which they were assigned, though over the years all sorts of scoundrels have been welcomed with a flourish. Rejection or expulsion was rare until the Cold War, when ambassadors and their staffs, some of whom were exposed as dandified spies, were sent packing in tit-for-tat flurries.

The United States did not get around to sending full ambassadors abroad, or accepting them, until 1893—more than a century after the nation's founding. Ministers, operating from legations, had previously been the highest-ranking American diplomats. Congress, just starting to recognize the nation's role as a world power, nonetheless had to be talked into posting ambassadors and sent them only to leading European and three Latin American nations. The first full ambassador from another country to present credentials to a president was Sir Julian Pauncefote of Great Britain, who beat the French ambassador to Grover Cleveland's White House by a single day. His was also the first government to buy or build a residence for its Washington representative—a brick house on Connecticut Avenue. "It is a hideous object outside," wrote *The Illustrated American* magazine, "but, like many other houses, and even individuals, the inner house is beautiful."

It would be wrong to say that our rambunctious new democracy did not envision itself as a diplomatic destination. The excitable dreamer who laid out the Plan of Washington, the Frenchman Pierre-Charles L'Enfant, pictured a "vast esplanade," worthy of Versailles, to be cleared from the Potomac thicket and along which "all such sort of places as may be attractive to the learned and afford diversion to the idle" might be located. Foreign legations were chief among this "sort of places." Instead, governments kept their distance from what was a pestiferous, brambly eyesore, and the Mall became a jumble of storehouses and railroad sheds before it was rehabilitated in the "City Beautiful" movement that swept the nation following the 1893 Chicago world's fair.

The first envoy to American shores was Conrad Alexander Gérad, who was appointed "minister plenipotentiary" in 1778—a year after France became the first nation to recognize the independence of Britain's 13 colonies, even though the war for freedom was still raging. Soon after the new United States settled upon the bumptious capital upstream from President George Washington's Mount Vernon home, the government sent notices to France, England, Spain, Portugal, and the Netherlands that it would be pleased to provide convenient sites along L'Enfant's proposed esplanade on which to "accommodate you agreeably." There were no takers. The foreign ministers who had dared take up residence in this callow country had found tolerable comfort in Philadelphia and saw no advantage to moving. When the relocation became official, the French minister asked for and was granted indefinite home leave in preference to a barbarous assignment in a miasmal bog.

In 1800, a week before President and Mrs. John Adams arrived to take up residence in the White House, Britain's George Hammond moved to town. So repulsed was he that he, too, soon sailed away, leaving the mission in the hands of an unfortunate chargé d'affaires. For almost a year after John and Abigail Adams set up housekeeping, only the Spanish minister, Llosa Ojeda, listed a Washington address, and he found excuses to spend most of his tour in Philadelphia and New York.

The city's first Embassy Row was actually a single abode—Decatur House on Lafayette Square, now a property of the National Trust for Historic Preservation. Designed by Benjamin Latrobe, who worked on both the Capitol and the White House, it was owned by Admiral Stephen Decatur until his death in a duel. His widow then rented out rooms to the representatives of various nations. Baron de Tuyll, the minister from imperial Russia, was Mrs. Decatur's bête noire. According to an article by the *Washington Post*'s Sarah Booth Conroy, written in 1976, "He built a greenhouse which caused her insurance to be canceled, and one of his servants tried to bill her for furniture he bought."

For the better part of a century, Washington was universally maligned as a hardship post, on the order of Rangoon or Timbuktu, with pay differentials to match. (It would remain a hardship post for black African diplomats well into the 20th century, as they sought equitable treatment in a segregated city.) In the earliest days of the capital, only the low in rank or the high in disfavor spent the summer in town. The Dutch ambassador arrived in 1801 but, according to Hope Ridings Miller in *Embassy Row,* "left the following year, complaining about the rigors of living in a frontier country." It would be 13 years before the Dutch bothered to send a replacement.

Miller tells the story of Sir Charles Bagot, the first British minister after the War of 1812, who had been counseled before arriving, "The problem confronting you is not so much what you can do in America, but how much you can bear." As it developed, he could bear little. "There is no enjoyment here," he wrote. "All I can hope to do is to prevent being unhappy, and that I shall manage by looking forward, or upward, or backward—any way but Yankeeward."

L'Enfant's magnificent radials were one thing on a map, quite another in reality for a century or more. Downtown streets were an odiferous morass when it rained, a choking slog of powdery dust when it did not. Nearly everything north of Florida Avenue—then fittingly called Boundary Street—was a "suburb" of verdant glens to which the gentry escaped by carriage and later streetcar to drink the purifying water, breathe agreeable air, check into sanitariums, or frolic at amusement parks. The part of the District of Columbia north of Boundary Street was not even in L'Enfant's original Washington City; it was called Washington County. When former Union general and U.S. Senator John Brooks Henderson built his three-story, red-sandstone "castle" at Florida Avenue and 16th Street in 1888, it pushed the limits of refined civilization north into the wilderness. Between 1906 and 1929, his wife (and widow as of 1913), Mary Foote Henderson, commissioned architect George Oakley Totten to construct a dozen palatial residences around nearby Meridian Hill, on which she sought to build a new presidential residence far grander than the White House. Failing that, she thought the Lincoln Memorial would look splendid nearby. Architects designed both, but Congress demurred. Finally she settled for a lovely park containing a memorial to President James Buchanan, a bronze statue of Dante, and an equestrian treatment of Joan of Arc. Wealthy industrialists, who had made their fortunes providing goods to the growing nation, bought or leased the grandiose Totten homes, such as the Pink Palace at 2600 16th Street, as second homes in Washington. Takers, too, were foreign governments, finally acknowledging the first-tier status of the United States. In the newspapers of the 1920s, 16th Street began to be known as Embassy Row.

Massachusetts Avenue, or rather the portion of Washington's longest thoroughfare from Scott Circle to Wisconsin Avenue, would wrest the title a decade later when the British built their new multimillion-dollar headquarters on "Massachusetts Avenue extended." Like 16th Street, the avenue had once been bucolic countryside, a favorite haunt of sports seekers. An 1809 city council "Act to Prevent Swine from Going at Large" set Massachusetts Avenue as the absolute boundary of citification. But after District of Columbia Governor Alexander "Boss" Shepherd graded and landscaped the avenue in the 1870s, it became a magnet for socialite expansion. Some of the city's first large-scale land speculators, the California Syndicate that included silver magnate and U.S. Senator William Stewart, gobbled up land west of Dupont Circle. Wealthy entrepreneurs, drawn to Washington to exert influence and further social ambitions, outdid one another in retaining architects and commissioning homes. The gas lamps of Massachusetts Avenue and Kalorama Heights mansions burned long into the night as the elite took turns celebrating their good fortune. When that fortune faded for many in the Great Depression—and when Uncle Sam began collecting income taxes—many of the barons of business left their drafty in-town mansions for less expensive, secluded homes in pastoral Maryland and Virginia. Soon the nouveau riche were establishing a beachhead on the avenue with smaller-scale places of their own; some of Embassy Row's great homes fell before the wrecker's crane, and others were converted to apartments or clubs. But several estates moved into the hands of foreign legations, which had been looking for fashionable elbow room and could afford to keep mansions out of the clutches of both subdividers and "revenuers," because they could not be taxed.

As the world's roster of countries raced past 100 and Washington's prestige as the capital of the free world soared, embassies of every size, resource, and geopolitical persuasion clustered as close to the old Embassy Row as their budgets would allow. Surprisingly, almost no diplomatic missions were located in now-fashionable Georgetown, which was considered a long haul from the White House and was somewhat seedy around the edges until the New Deal. A few embassies ventured farther afield, some into the business section of town but more than a few, illegally, into residential neighborhoods, to the consternation of inhabitants. Washington had become a plum rather than a hardship assignment. "A stay in Washington is considered very precipitous [sic] for our future career," Japanese embassy attaché Hiroaki Fujii told the *Washington Post* in 1979. After a tour of the new Japanese ambassador's home in 1978, the *Post*'s Conroy noted, "In Washington, embassies are our modern-day palaces, marble manifestations of the way the nations of the world wish to present themselves to other countries." So insatiable has been the diplomatic community's search for office space that the U.S. State Department publishes a fancy manual on acquiring foreign missions. It is shaped like an elongated U.S. passport, complete with a fake-leather cover and embossed State Department seal.

It was not until the 1950s that the first woman envoy arrived in Washington—Madame Vijaya Lakshmi Pandit, India's ambassador and sister of the then prime minister, Jawaharlal Nehru—and not until 1970 that the Executive Protective Service, the uniformed arm of the Secret

A baroque-style wood organ is built into the wall of the Indonesian embassy's music room, whose coffered ceiling is divided by dark beams into gilded ornamental panels.

15

Service, began patrolling diplomatic buildings. These measures were undertaken in response to increasingly combative demonstrations whose targets fluctuated with world events. Embassies of South Africa, the Soviet Union, Iran, Israel, Nicaragua, South Korea, and South Vietnam have been frequent objectives of protesters over the years. In 1988 the U.S. Supreme Court struck down a District of Columbia ban on demonstrations within 500 feet of an embassy, ruling that it violated the First Amendment right of free speech. The presence of Executive Protective Service guards also cut reported crime at embassies, which had included burglaries, stolen limousines, and several bombings. One crime that was planned but never happened: a proposal by the National Security Agency in the early 1970s to break into foreign embassies to steal their spy codes; Federal Bureau of Investigation Director J. Edgar Hoover nixed the idea "because of the risk," according to top-secret documents leaked to the press.

Many Washingtonians argue that the spread of embassies and chanceries—with their antenna nests, fleets of cars with diplomatic plates, claims on parking spaces, and renovations that turn lofty old mansions into office complexes—has been a blot on city neighborhoods. As early as 1945, *Nation's Business* estimated that 40,000 representatives were crowding into Washington, doing the work of foreign governments. By 1983 the city's 145 foreign missions and 23 international organizations owned 375 separate facilities around the city. In the early 1960s Congress and the city tried to slip a discrete chancery zone into Chevy Chase; howling neighbors' phone calls helped kill the scheme. Senator J. William Fulbright, who owned a house in the Sheridan-Kalorama section of the city, fielded numerous complaints about chancery sprawl, and Congress in the mid-1960s passed what became known as the Fulbright Amendment, restricting the expansion of new diplomatic facilities to high-density commercial or "mixed-use" zones.

In 1977 the National Capital Planning Commission published a comprehensive plan for missions and international agencies, and a year later Congress established a separate Office of Foreign Missions in the Department of State, in part to keep a rein on the skimble-skamble growth of chanceries. The planning commission went so far as to draw up blueprints for a chancery enclave near George Washington University Hospital in the Foggy Bottom section of the district, but congressional intervention once again scuttled the plan. The chancery-glut issue was finally somewhat ameliorated in the 1980s with the creation of an imposing International Center on 22 acres of federal land at the old National Bureau of Standards site at Connecticut Avenue and Van Ness Street uptown. By the early 1990s the chanceries of Austria, Bahrain, Ghana, Israel, Jordan, and Kuwait had located there. At the same time, construction began (and most likely will continue through much of the decade) on the last piece of the downtown Federal Triangle, the International Cultural and Trade Center, in what had been the Triangle's Great Plaza. The ICTC, the second largest federal building in the United States (after the Pentagon), was designed in part to accommodate foreign trade and cultural offices.

Embassies have come, gone, and sometimes come again. Few who worked diplomatic Washington in 1941 could forget the sight of smoke rising from the chimney of the German embassy, where the fine ashes of secret papers were rising skyward as the embassy prepared to close. "I must leave my horse, Kitty-Charr," the German ambassador's wife, Frau Annelsie Thomsen, regretfully told the *Washington Post.* "Also, I hate to leave all my little pets—I have 86 of them—squirrels, flying squirrels and birds. What will they do when I am not here to feed them?" She vowed to return after the war to renew friendships. "I wish all of you a merry, merry Christmas. Goodby."

The conduct of embassy affairs isn't all that upsets some locals' sensibilities. So does the off-the-job behavior of the diplomatic entourage. In 1990, for instance, a moonlighting Kuwait embassy messenger, stopped by metropolitan police, had to be reminded that delivering pizza in a car bearing embassy plates was out of diplomatic bounds. Over the years, higher-ranking envoys have also found themselves in embarrassing scrapes, including shoplifting incidents and auto accidents, from which only diplomatic immunity saved them. In 1962 the *Washington Star* even editorialized about the "disgraceful performance" of a Belgian air attaché, Colonel Maurice Schwarz, who had rammed another vehicle with his car, inflicting $500 in damage. "It is gratifying," wrote the *Star,* "that the State Department has taken special note of the affair, is investigating the circumstances, and has reminded all foreign diplomats that the shield of immunity is not broad enough to relieve them of responsibility to respect local laws and the rights of others. . . . It would be well to keep an eye on Colonel Schwarz in the future. If there is a repetition of anything of this sort he should be shipped home in a hurry." Straightening out such peccadilloes is a part of the turf of an entire State Department bureaucracy, the Office of Protocol.

The Spanish embassy was one of a dozen villas designed by architect George Oakley Totten as part of Mary Foote Henderson's plan for a grand diplomatic neighborhood carved from the 16th Street wilderness.

Today as always, the meat and potatoes of embassies' work involves assisting their nationals, issuing visas, dispensing business and travel information, representing their nations to the president and his officers, and conducting carefully choreographed exchanges among themselves. Statesmanlike tedium is the price the representative to Washington pays, but there is a most satisfactory trade-off. As Thomas Bailey pointed out in the 1940 *History of the American People,* the business of diplomacy is entertainment, "just as it is of the traveling salesman. The more people the ambassador ingratiates himself with, the better he can do his job. Many an important bit of information is dropped over the fourth cocktail. . . . Cynics have defined a diplomat as an 'honest man sent to lie abroad for his country.' He might perhaps better be defined as 'a man sent abroad to dine for his country,' sometimes on stewed cat."

Eric Sevareid and Robert A. Smith, in their 1965 book, *Washington: Magnificent Capital,* called diplomats "Washington's cosmopolitan night people": "With spidery unobtrusiveness, they form invisible webs of personal contacts, spinning gossamer strands of goodwill with a handshake, an embrace, an exchange of pleasantries, a whispered confidence, a raised glass, ingratiating themselves throughout the diplomatic, military, and political communities, snaring choice morsels of intelligence for the home office."

In this convivial milieu, especially during the social season from November through February, balancing a guest list becomes an art form, phrasing a toast or choosing a wine a tour de force. Indeed, the raconteurial renown of some former ambassadors is still remembered. So esteemed was one dean of the corps, the Frenchman Jules Jusserand, who regaled Washington from 1902 to 1925, that a plaque commemorating his service, presented at his farewell dinner, was placed in Rock Creek Park.

Balls, receptions, and trips past Washington's greatest groaning boards are standard diplomatic activities. First among equals on the social circuit are Holland's Tulip Festival, Sweden's Santa Lucia Christmas repast, national independence day celebrations at numerous embassies, strawberries and cream and toasts to the queen's birthday at the British embassy, Columbus Day festivities, and the French commemoration of Bastille Day. The most elegant of all diplomatic do's is the annual White House reception, first made glamorous by John and Jacqueline Kennedy.

But many embassy events serve a nobler purpose than the displaying of new finery. Harking back to World War II "Bundles for Britain" soirees and French Red Cross receptions are the annual embassy tours, which give the inquisitive public a peek inside these glamorous quarters, with admission fees going to various charities. One of the first tours, in the early 1940s, benefited the Washington Home for the Incurables, but the most enduring has been a springtime fixture of Goodwill Industries. The Goodwill Guild's first affair, in 1947, drew 500 ladies in hats and gloves and netted Goodwill $800; Bess Truman was a hostess for the concluding tea. Now the Goodwill Embassy Tour and Gala cut off ticket sales at 3,000.

So intense was one Washingtonian's curiosity about the elusive workings of an embassy that she wrote to *Washington Daily News* columnist Evelyn Peyton Gordon in 1947, asking how she might get invited to a reception. "It's not such a difficult problem, my dear lady," replied Gordon, who advised her to get some "visiting cards" correctly engraved, "wear your best clothes and gloves," and set forth, leaving cards at chosen residences. "If the envoy has a wife, two cards should be left — a Mr. and Mrs. card for the diplomat and his wife, and a Mr. card for the envoy. A woman never calls on a man. An unmarried man leaves

Tiles from Puebla, Mexico, laid in 1937 at the Mexican Cultural Institute, depict the shields of the Mexican states and a view of the ancient cities of Popocatepetl and Ixtacihvatt.

two of his cards, and a single woman leaves one card for the madame. Unfortunately an unmarried woman can not call on a bachelor envoy." *Cosmopolitan* magazine reported the outrage, in 1901, that followed the arrival at the Mexican embassy of a mother with "a brood of dirty children." They barged into the ballroom, and after settling the youngsters on a French-upholstered divan, the woman "proceeded to the dining-room and helped herself to enough cake to satisfy the ravenous youngsters. It is hardly to be wondered at, therefore, that to give a public entertainment is not regarded as a pleasure by the foreign Embassies, and the decline of this form of function has been very rapid." Public tours of embassies are indeed rare today, more for reasons of security than of propriety.

An article published in 1958 in *Better Homes and Gardens* magazine divulged the strict schedule governing an ambassador's formal dinners: "Guests are invited for 8 p.m., and are expected to be no more than five minutes late. At 10:45 p.m., the ranking guest is supposed to leave, whereupon everybody else may then leave if they like. If it is an extremely good party, sometimes the ranking guest will depart, take a walk around the block, and return. This ploy, it seems, automatically cancels all protocol about protocol."

The sashaying side to diplomacy, the elegant repasts with starchy conventions and vacuous conversations have provoked the sharpest barbs. From the late United Nations ambassador and presidential candidate Adlai Stevenson: "A diplomat's life is made up of three ingredients: protocol, Geritol, and alcohol." Actor Peter Ustinov: "A diplomat these days is nothing but a headwaiter who's allowed to sit down occasionally." And the late Italian writer and diplomat Daniele Vare: "Diplomacy is the art of letting someone else have your way."

In 1984 novelist Sondra Gotlieb, wife of the then Canadian ambassador, wrote in the *Washington Post* about the visit of "Popsie Tribble," who "drops in every six weeks or so to tell me how to conduct my life in Washington." Popsie brought a list of do's (hire a butler who can announce the guests by their right names) and don'ts (avoid pregnant maids). Popsie and Sondra looked in on the kitchen and found the new Bulgarian chef with "a tumbler in one hand while he basted some ducks with the other.

"Popsie said loudly, 'I think you should fire him.'

"'Don't you think I should wait till after dinner?' I whispered. 'There are thirty people coming this evening.'

"'Maybe that's wise,' she agreed, and we went upstairs."

In 1956 *Washington Star* society columnist Betty Beale listed some of the pet peeves of "party-trotting women" who frequented the embassy scene. The greatest affront of all: coat-checkers' "cozy little custom of leaving a dish out with coins in it in hopes of getting more. To have to pay to get your own garments back at a private party is certainly the ne plus ultra of the bottom drawer!"

In 1973 *Washington Post* writer Henry Mitchell devoted some space to a comparison of canapés at various embassy affairs. He described the "peculiarly excellent" Swedish meatballs at the Dutch embassy and strawberries "at their peak" at the Belgian embassy during the daffodil season, but "mealy and often hollow" at the Japanese embassy. "But things even out," he wrote. "The Japanese melon balls were great." Had Mitchell made the circuit several decades earlier, during the Great Depression, he'd have been caustic indeed. So grim was the international stock and banking crisis that cocktails were served without olives, liquor was rationed, and sea water substituted for gin. Many envoys served at nominal wages or without pay for the duration.

Until the 1980s, the typical society-page coverage of an embassy event consisted of an opening paragraph describing the time, place, and nature of the affair, followed by several columns listing each and every guest and what he—and especially she—wore. Every word was flattering, at least at first read. A typical entry was Hazel Markel's notation in a 1951 issue of *The Diplomat:* "Mme. Henri Bonnet receiving for famed Gen. Jean de Lattre de Tassigny, wearing Christian Dior's stunning emerald-toned taffeta, a low cut bodice, a side-swept crinolined skirt and yards on yards of dotted white chiffon stole." The columnists' colleagues in the feature section were not always so saccharine.

Early on, the typical ambassador's attire sported epaulets and medals; some men turned down important foreign posts because they could not keep up appearances. Fashion plates in the diplomatic corps wore hussar capes, Turkish fezzes, diamond-encrusted turbans, Oriental silks, a variety of Knights Templar uniforms, and, reported *Cosmopolitan* in 1901, coats with "frogs and slashes" and "astrakhan-trimmed chapeaux with black feather tufts." It was during the presidency of Andrew Jackson, who ran with a coonskin-cap crowd, that "the simple dress of an American citizen," occasionally augmented by a sword, would be fine for Washington's diplomatic gentlemen. Years later, a standard business suit by day and dinner jacket by night became the uniform. Titled noblemen, who once dominated Washington diplomacy, were a rarity by 1935, when only 19 of 431 envoys were to the manner born. One, however, the British ambassador, Sir Ronald Lindsay, had a string of 12 honorary initials (P.C., G.C.M.G., K.C.B., C.V.O.) trailing after his name.

The duties of these envoys have rarely been described as arduous. "There is work enough to keep the blood from stagnating in most houses, perhaps," wrote the *Star* in 1928, "but when breakfast has been eaten, the diplomat has before him a pleasant afternoon and evening."

Making a good impression and unraveling misunderstandings are two of the envoy's responsibilities. "Being an ambassador these days is a bit like being an airline stewardess," Henry Catto, then U.S. ambassador to the Court of St. James and later director of the United States Information Agency, told *Washingtonian* magazine in 1991. "You serve many meals, and you clean up minor messes." Forty years earlier, writer Robley D. Stevens pointed out in an article on embassy public relations in *The Diplomat,* "[The ambassador] must win the confidence of the American people. . . . He should talk a 'plain' language—discuss the affairs of his country as related to the American scene without hesitancy. Nothing will win Americans more quickly than the knowledge that the 'man at the top' is a 'regular fellow' and that he also has problems."

The Diplomat was a chichi publication produced from 1941 to 1966, based in Washington but catering to the gentility on the go worldwide. Washington's embassies themselves got scant treatment, but the comings and goings of their ambassadors were lavishly covered. "The great 'Whispering Gallery' that is our nation's capital reverberates with rumors of what goes on in the Inner Circle and speculations as to Who will be Who here after November," wrote a columnist in 1964. *The Diplomat's* regular features, tucked amid advertising for furriers, cruise lines, violin studios, and Cadillac dealerships, included seasonal updates from the Hamptons, Bermuda, Nassau, and Palm Beach. Debs from Dallas to Philadelphia got coverage. The diplomatic set read about "leg loveliness for summer," "male plumage," and "matching lips and nails." Regular columns included "Confessions of a Grand Duke" and "Celebrities at Play."

In its December 1953 tip on protocol, *The Diplomat* informed the haut monde how to address an ambassador properly: "'His excellency' is the complimentary title. . . . Personal titles, such as 'Baron,' 'Count,' 'Jonkheer,' etc., which are indications of rank or intimately associated with certain foreign names, are to be added."

Such flowery discourse gets shorter shrift today. "Society" columns of newspapers have given way to "Style" or "Living" sections that glorify more rock musicians and film stars than debutantes. Hope Ridings Miller, who was the *Washington Post* society editor for seven years, once, in a blue moment, wrote a column titled "Farewell to Society." "What's killed it," she told the authors of this book, "is that they [the society set] can't get publicity any more. That's important to the 'climbers,' and it's important to the embassies, in order to justify their 'representational funds,' the funds for entertainment. They still give parties; they're just not written up as much. But, believe me, next to an invitation to the White House, an embassy invitation still rates."

Nowadays, issues far graver than who sits to the right of the host occupy the ambassador posted to Washington. Complexities of trade, long-simmering ethnic resentments inside and among nations, even overnight changes in ideology have encumbered the diplomat's job. Who could have foreseen the day when delirious mobs would topple statues of Lenin and snip the hammer and sickle from national flags? Even with such dizzying complications, however, when the sun dips below the Potomac and the first drinks are served or the first dance announced, the magic of cultivated conversation, well-bred courtliness, and exquisite fashion still shimmers inside these residences. It is into this unflappable world that *Embassies of Washington* invites you.

The Red Living Room at the Spanish ambassador's residence showcases a rug created at the Real Fabrica de Tapices in Madrid. Following pages: The Belgian ambassador's house is a faithful reproduction of the Hôtel de Charolais in Paris.

┈┈┈┈┈┈╒╗║╚┈┈┈┈┈

RESIDENCE OF THE
AMBASSADOR OF BELGIUM

Baker's Acres

2300 Foxhall Road, Northwest

Horace Trumbauer, Architect

════ 1931 ════

*Up to 30 guests can
enjoy legendary cuisine
in the Belgian ambas-
sador's dining room.
The gold-trimmed
white china bears the
Belgian seal; the crystal
is Val St. Lambert.*

IN 1931 THE *WASHINGTON DAILY NEWS* REPORTED that "one of the most widely known figures in society, both in America and in Europe" was about to build a $310,000 home to occupy "the entire 2300 block of Foxhall Road nw." That dapper figure was Raymond T. Baker, a onetime Nevada gold prospector, prison warden, and Reno bank president who had served as private secretary to the U.S. ambassador to Russia and as Woodrow Wilson's secretary of the Mint. His new house rose on Baker's Acres, so dubbed, in part, because it covered 13 (a baker's dozen) acres.

The limestone château, which a *Washington Star* reviewer would call "a petit palais at the edge of the woods," is an accurate reproduction of the Hôtel de Charolais in Paris. Its specifications, remarkable for the time, included a cold-storage room for rugs and furs, a refrigeration room for cut flowers, and a storage chamber specially designed to closet bottled water. Crystal chandeliers, Aubusson carpets, parquet floors, and carved paneling were imported from France. Philadelphia architect Horace Trumbauer, whose work included that city's Ritz-Carlton Hotel, paid special attention to the wide rear terrace, which offers a vista of the Virginia countryside across the Potomac River. In the opposite direction, across Foxhall Road, was another expanse of woods soon to be filled by a second legendary estate, on which storied Washington hostess and philanthropist Gwendolyn Cafritz would site her 15,000-square-foot Art Moderne home.

The Bakers' neighbor down the road was Mrs. J. Borden Harriman, whose Terrace Heights estate had been built two years earlier. According to Hope Ridings Miller in *The Great Houses of Washington*, Daisy Harriman and Delphine Baker were fast friends and fellow Democratic Party shakers, but their friendship did not deter Daisy Harriman from suing the Bakers for $15,000 when workers clearing Baker's Acres dumped 15 tons of dirt onto Harriman land. The parties quietly settled out of court.

Baker, whom an obituary called "a man with an attractive personality, with a natural gift for making friends among all sorts of people," married well, first to Margaret Emerson, heiress to the Bromo-Seltzer fortune, then to Delphine Dodge Cromwell of the Detroit automobile family. (The first Mrs. Baker took her divorce in stride, proceeding to marry Alfred Gwynne Vanderbilt.) Baker died in the house within four years of its christening.

The French Renaissance home remained a hub of social gaiety, however. It was leased by Dwight F. Davis, who had served as secretary of war, and then by the queen of Palm Beach Society, Mrs. Edward T. Stotesbury. According to Hope Miller, one of Mrs. Stotesbury's most memorable soirees was set for December 7, 1941, a few hours "after the jaw-shivering news of Pearl Harbor hit Washington. Foreign emissaries, high State Department officials, and enough members of the House and Senate to pass a congressional bill were in the distressed throng that milled through the mansion's salons that evening."

In 1945 the Baker house, as it was still known, was sold to the Belgian government, which was desperately seeking larger embassy

quarters. Belgian war-supply efforts had been conducted out of rooms at the old embassy on Massachusetts Avenue.

But the entertainment schedule at Baker's Acres hardly skipped a beat. Baron Robert Silvercruys and his successor, Baron Louis M. Scheyven, were both connoisseurs of decorative arts. Baron Scheyven, who had held diplomatic posts throughout the world, installed silver plates from Egypt, icons from Russia and Germany, ivory bulls from China, and a wooden madonna and infant from his homeland. The embassy library—a replica of the one presented by the late J. Pierpont

Morgan to the Metropolitan Museum of Art in New York—seated 50 and was dominated by a flamboyant scarlet phoenix, emblem of the Chinese empress. The wife of a French ambassador to the United States remarked that the Louis XVI salon was "the most beautiful room in Washington."

Baron Scheyven, a gourmet, was fond of recalling that he "learned something about food" when he steamed to China as a galley boy on a Pacific liner. One of his sumptuous repasts is recalled in *Embassy Row* as meeting "the last word in excellence," attesting to the adage "The French cuisine is good; the Belgian is divine." It should be noted, however, that the Belgian national meat dish is biftek, which the book *Diplomatic Dishes* says is "usually prepared with ox, calf, pig, or horse."

On November 15, 1974, Ambassador Willy Van Cauwenberg got a chuckle from the 750 guests at his first big reception on "the occasion of The King's Day." It turned out not to be King Baudouin's birthday, which was September 7, nor the Belgians' national day,

which is July 21. An embassy official interpolated that it must be "St. Leopold's Day," safe in the knowledge that there had been three King Leopolds. But a prankish guest quick-checked a history book and found no correlation with any of the Leopolds. By evening's end, the invitees had settled on a celebration of the birthday of St. Albert, predecessor to one of the Leopolds.

The Belgians also once earned a titter when an embassy secretary maintained, unsuccessfully, that her pet ocelots Sabu and Elizabeth had diplomatic immunity and should not be confiscated.

But most of the attention focuses on the graceful château itself and its contents. The Hauteville marble floor and post-impressionist Taf Wallet paintings in the entrance hall, the replica of a library of natural-finished oak designed by Georges Hoentschel, drawing-room tapestries woven after cartoons by the Belgian painter Edgard Tytgat, and hand-made Belgian crystal throughout the house are among the city's most remarkable furnishings.

Lush gardens, once the pride of Delphine Dodge Baker, second wife of the director of the U.S. Mint, grace the Belgian ambassador's home. A sunny informal Garden Room opens onto it.

THE GLOBE-TROTTING DAUGHTER OF THE FOUNDER
of the *Chicago Tribune,* married to the former U.S. ambassador to Austria-
Hungary, then Russia, and then France, could afford a fancy address for
the couple's new home in Washington. Katherine Medill McCormick
bought an imposing triangular corner of Pretty Prospect along Massachusetts Avenue, part of the Rock of Dumbarton property north of
Georgetown, and hired John Russell Pope to create a new home for her
and her husband, Robert, that would provide a proper setting for the
collection of exquisite furnishings the McCormicks had acquired in their
far-ranging travels. Pope—the man destined to become one of America's
great Classical Revival architects—would later design three of Washington's most imposing structures: the National Gallery of Art, the National Archives building, and the Jefferson Memorial. He was already
thinking big when he went to work on the McCormick mansion.

Katherine's husband, "Colonel" Robert McCormick—the isola-
tionist publisher of the *Tribune* and the *Washington Times-Herald*—died in
1919, and five years later Mrs. McCormick deeded the house and land
(for $10) and the "furniture, pictures, draperies, rugs, tapestries, bric-a-
brac, objects of art, and household furnishings of every kind" (for another $10) to her son, U.S. Senator Medill McCormick. Yet Mother Mc-
Cormick, and not the senator, kept the house as a Washington address
when she was not back in Chicago or avidly touring abroad; indeed, she
would die in a hotel in Versailles. Her son, the senator, died in 1925, and
his widow, Ruth (herself the daughter of Senator Mark Hanna), made
a run for his seat; she won the Republican nomination but lost the elec-
tion. At Katherine McCormick's death in 1931, title to the Massachusetts
Avenue mansion reverted to her daughter-in-law. Ruth also inherited
Katherine's furs and laces. A *New York Times* article about Katherine Mc-
Cormick's estate noted that "Mrs. McCormick made it clear in her will
that all the contents of her house at 3000 Massachusetts Avenue were
the property of her son, Medill McCormick, and are now the property
of Mrs. Simms." "Mrs. Simms" was Ruth McCormick Simms, who had
married New Mexico Congressman Albert G. Simms a year after her
mother-in-law's death. In 1934 the Simmses sold the mansion to "The
United States of Brazil" for $200,000, following what a Brazilian publi-
cation called "intense negotiations." Albert and Ruth then moved back
to Illinois—turf of the Medills and McCormicks—where Ruth became
publisher of two newspapers in Rockford.

With the purchase of the McCormick house, Brazil became the
second nation, after Great Britain, to locate an embassy on Massachusetts Avenue. The Brazilians modified the downstairs, turning the
library into a state dining room and eliminating several service rooms.
A year later, on land they bought next door along Whitehaven Street
from the McCormick estate for another $50,000, they erected a
chancery—replaced by a modern structure in 1971.

A slick, 46-page brochure published by the embassy in 1986,
somewhat belatedly marking the 50th anniversary of its government's
purchase of the McCormick house, recalls that embassy affairs had previously been conducted in a variety of cramped locations in northwest

RESIDENCE OF THE
AMBASSADOR OF BRAZIL
McCormick House
3000 Massachusetts Avenue, Northwest
John Russell Pope, Architect
—— *1910* ——

Washington. An earlier embassy publication, this one from 1935, described the situation: "Some distinguished visitors felt ashamed, sad-
dened and disheartened when they saw the hovel leased at a high rent
to house the Mission. The Brazilian Embassy provided painful and hu-
miliating contrast to the Embassies and even with some Legations." So
Ambassador Oswaldo Aranha—in Brazil at the time of Katherine Mc-
Cormick's death but soon to be appointed ambassador to Washington—
persuaded his government to end the embarrassment of a leased home
and furnishings and buy the grand building.

    With some pride, the brochure's introduction concludes, "The
now-famous Embassy Row on Massachusetts Avenue, lined with
scores of Missions representing countries from five continents, began
with the Embassies of Brazil and Great Britain."

    The U.S. Commission of Fine Arts described the McCormicks'
Indiana limestone house as "a study in aloof elegance." (The Brazilian
brochure states that Pope's work is "characterized by neatness of exe-
cution and reserved elegance.") The Renaissance Revival house sits
back from Massachusetts Avenue and features a recessed entrance inspired by Peruzzi's Palazzo Massimo alle Colonne in Rome.

*Wallpaper in the
Brazilian ambassador's
Reception Room is
taken from Johann
Moritz Rugendas's
PAYSAGES DU BRÉSIL,
painted in 1830.
Opposite:
These objets d'art have
been gathered from
Europe and throughout
the Americas.*

29

WASHINGTON HAS CHOICE DIPLOMATIC LOCATIONS, but when Canada went looking for a new chancery site in the early 1980s, it got a prime one, four blocks from the Capitol on "America's Main Street." How did Canada pull it off? Being the United States' next-door neighbor, largest trading partner, and close ally helped. So did the fact that the American embassy in Ottawa sits across the street from Parliament. And so did some good horse-trading.

The District of Columbia owned the site that Canada had in mind—a generous plot on which sat a frumpy structure that had been built as a library and a former Ford assembly plant, where Henry Ford once unveiled the Model A. Diagonally across the street, I. M. Pei's modernist, trapezoidal National Gallery of Art East Wing was already looming. D.C. regulations stipulated that the city must receive fair-market value for the property, then assessed at $7 million, and the Canadians had budgeted only $4 million in U.S. currency. To the rescue came the agency that had been spiffing up whole chunks of the Avenue of the Presidents, the Pennsylvania Avenue Development Corporation, which tossed in $2 million to compensate for the Canadians' sacrifice of the mandated "setback" that would push the building far from the avenue. With a little arm-twisting, city officials settled for the $6 million.

British Columbia–born, Toronto-based architect Arthur Erickson—designer of cascading, often abstract buildings from Vancouver to Kuwait City and a winner of the American Institute of Architects' Gold Medal—went to work on the distinctive $30 million, 287,000-square-foot building. "One day, a spontaneous inner impulse triggers a reaction. . . . The idea [for a building], or child, emerges," he told *Washington Post* architecture critic Benjamin Forgey.

The building won praise from some quarters, derision from others. Some said that it "made a statement." Forgey loved it. "[It] is a mighty battleship of a building with a sharp prow aimed across the wide street," he wrote. "Behind the prow is a great rotunda in the open air, its twelve concrete columns . . . echoing the rounded classical revival terminus of the nearby Federal Trade Commission. [Erickson's] building is an edgy, flawed masterpiece . . . but a masterpiece." Indeed, the building represents an ingenious attempt at appropriating disparate themes from its neighbors—slashing edges from Pei's East Wing and the rounded stub of the FTC. However, the *New York Times*'s architecture critic, Paul Goldberger, called it a "curiously convoluted structure" that failed to blend well with the avenue's monumental style. An unsigned piece in Washington's *City Paper* called the building "a Late Modern nightmare" that, like The Thing in the horror movie of the same name, "has landed on Pennsylvania Avenue." Washington's architects, still in a swoon over the fortress-like intrusion of the J. Edgar Hoover FBI building five blocks up the avenue, eagerly contributed to the lively debate.

Soon after dedicating the Erickson building, the Canadian government sold its 1950s-era chancery and its ornate 1909 main embassy. For the hundreds of relocated employees, the new structure has offered several perks: a livelier downtown milieu and one of Washington's best views of Inauguration Day parades.

CHANCERY OF CANADA
*501 Pennsylvania Avenue, Northwest
Arthur Erickson, Architect*
1988

The marble Canadian embassy, in a choice location near the U.S. Capitol, includes a two-story Rotunda of the Provinces, described as a "perfect echo chamber" by embassy literature.

RESIDENCE OF THE
AMBASSADOR OF COLOMBIA

Gaff House

1520 20th Street, Northwest

J. Henri de Sibour, Architect

1906

*Midwest businessman
Thomas Gaff built
novel conveniences into
his new Washington
residence, but they are
well concealed in the
grand manor that
became the Colombian
ambassador's home.*

THE ECLECTIC TASTES OF THE INVENTIVE THOMAS
F. Gaff were evident in the new red-brick manor he was building for
himself and his wife, Zaidee, off Dupont Circle. A distiller and maker
of heavy machinery in Cincinnati, Gaff moved to Washington in 1906.
He hired architect Jules Henri de Sibour—a descendant of Louis
XVI who would subsequently design three other mansions that would
become residences of the ambassadors of France, Luxembourg, and
Portugal—to design his home. Among the practical features he included were the hot-air system for drying clothes, a trapdoor on his
icehouse (allowing direct delivery from the street), cork insulation for
the wine cellar, and a movable wooden wall that could close off the
domed Edwardian ballroom surmounted by a skylight. The dining
room included Elizabethan wainscoting and a sideboard from an Italian monastery.

     After Gaff died and his wife moved away, the house was leased
to several prominent Washingtonians, including President Calvin
Coolidge's secretary of war, Dwight F. Davis, and also to the governments of Greece and Colombia. In 1944 Colombia bought the building
from the Gaffs' daughter, Mrs. Cary D. Langhorne, who lived next door
on Q Street, for use as the Colombian ambassador's home.

32

CHANCERY AND RESIDENCE
OF THE AMBASSADOR
OF DENMARK

3200 Whitehaven Street, Northwest

Vilhelm Lauritzen, Architect

1960

*A painting of the
Danish Faroe Isles by
S. Havsteen-Mikkelsen
hangs above a library
couch and next to an
antique Bornholm clock.
Following pages:
A wall of ceramic birds
of Denmark executed
by sculptor Henrik
Starcke embellishes a
sunny open area.*

WHEN KING FREDERIK IX AND QUEEN INGRID OFFI-
cially opened their country's new embassy overlooking Rock Creek on
October 12, 1960, they welcomed the diplomatic world to a contemporary facility indeed. There was little pretense or swagger in Copenhagen
architect Vilhelm Lauritzen's utilitarian dual structures—chancery and
residence connected by a glass corridor. There was no epic colonnade,
no gabled mansard roof, no winding, conifer-shaded driveway. The
building fronts on a parking lot! The $1.3 million building incorporates
a stark vertical and horizontal array of marble and glass. According to
the editors of *Guide to the Architecture of Washington, D.C.,* published by
the local chapter of the American Institute of Architects, the building
"is cool, white, and almost crystalline against the wooded hill, but much
of its positive effect is lost when seen over a sea of polychromed tin"
from the automobiles parked out front.

The interior, too, is straight-lined and functional—"spare," the
Washington Post's Heidi L. Berry called it in a 1990 article. Even the
modern chandeliers that light nearly every room are similarly designed.
Various ambassadors and their wives have warmed the decor with trea-
sures—not so much from their tours around the world, as is the custom
of many envoys, but more often from the tiny North Sea nation itself.

NAVY CAPTAIN THOMAS MORAN HAD SERVED HIS country for 30 years when, in 1942, he got orders to ship out to San Juan, Puerto Rico, to become Tenth Naval District chief of staff. Moran, who lived on 24th Street, N.W., had already engaged architect Victor de Mers to build a new $65,000 Classical Revival house around the corner on Bancroft Place. He and his wife, Elma, were fixtures in the Washington social scene, but duty called. The house went up and stayed in his family for two years. Immediately after its completion in 1942, the ashlar limestone house, combining 18th-century French and

RESIDENCE OF THE
AMBASSADOR OF ECUADOR
Moran House
2320 Bancroft Place, Northwest
Victor de Mers, Architect
═══ 1942 ═══

English touches and featuring an oval interior hall, skylight, and graceful staircase leading to balcony landings on its two upper stories, was conferred the Washington Board of Trade award for municipal art. Two years later, the embassy of Ecuador, which occupied one of several Henderson homes on 15th Street, bought the Bancroft Place house as a residence for Ambassador and Señora Galo Plaza.

The house was empty when the Ecuadorians bought it, so it became a two-year decorating challenge. Finally, gold damask draperies, silver candelabras, chairs made of coral, as well as Ecuadorian cuisine such as *locro* cheese soup and potato-and-egg *llapingachos* drenched in peanut and cheese sauce, and countless hangings and flowers in the national colors of red, blue, and yellow greeted guests at the ambassador's housewarming. Subsequent ambassadors added artifacts dating back to the Incas, leather trunks and saddles, a Louis XV marble chimneypiece, crystal chandeliers, and Ecuadorian paintings and dolls.

Ambassador Plaza fascinated everyone who met him. A onetime member of his nation's soccer team, he switched to American football at the University of California but gave it up to immerse himself in learning the English language. Writing in the *Washington Star* in 1971, Newbold Noyes, Jr., marveled, "He learned to think—even to dream—with equal fluency in either language."

On his days at Georgetown University, to which he had switched in order to study diplomacy while working as an embassy attaché, Plaza told Noyes, "I was the greatest guy in the world. I had a coon-skin coat and a Chrysler. I also had diplomatic access to plenty of good liquor. My popularity in the younger set was phenomenal."

His father, an Ecuadorian general, detached him from his Chrysler and sent him to New York City to learn "real" work, just as the 1929 stock-market crash plunged the United States into prolonged depression. Plaza sold New Jersey real estate for free meals. He quit the real estate job, he told reporter Noyes, "when I found out the customers came along only because they got free lunches, too." So he sold calendars, but "the market petered out after the first of January." Out of money, Plaza, like millions of others, sold apples on the street to earn a cup of coffee. A stranger walked up to him one day, announced he recognized him as General Plaza's son, and offered him a job as assistant purser on a Grace Line ship to South America. Later, his father would rise to the Ecuadorian presidency, and Señor Plaza would become mayor of Quito. His diplomatic career was in motion.

Over many years and several incumbents, the Ecuadorian ambassador's residence became a favorite stop on the embassy tour and an occasional destination of Washington schoolchildren as part of an "embassy adoption" program once sponsored by the city's public school system. Each young visitor would bring along an essay. "Ecuador is near the equator; that's how it got its name," wrote one 10-year-old in 1979. "And they have bullfights," someone else offered. The children discovered that Panama hats actually come from Ecuador and that, as embassy-adoption program director Linda Johnson told them, "the world is our classroom."

Preceding pages:
A wrought-iron and gilt banister graces the oval-shaped central hall in the Ecuadorian ambassador's residence. A colonial wooden chest features brass bells, suspended by rawhide and iron chains, and a statue of the "Apocalyptic" Virgin.

RESIDENCE OF THE
AMBASSADOR OF EGYPT

Beale House
2301 Massachusetts Avenue, Northwest
Glenn Brown, Architect

1909

IF YOU'RE EVER OF A MIND TO MEASURE THE OUT-
side dimensions of the Egyptian ambassador's residence, be sure your
straightedge is flexible, because the Massachusetts Avenue facade is
gracefully rounded in Roman Revival style. When architect Glenn
Brown designed this stucco and limestone house for Margaret K. C.
Beale in 1909, he featured a central arch above the doorway at the third-
floor level, supported by columns from the second.

The Egyptian government bought the building in 1928 and trans-
formed a first-floor kitchen and servants' area into a Museum of Antiquities. This became a "must" stop on Goodwill Industries–sponsored
tours in the days when security concerns were less obsessive. A high-
light was a collection of mummified sacred birds of the pharaohs, such
as the ibis and hawk—fitting for a nation that was a center of ancient
civilization. Objects dating as far back as 3,000 B.C. were augmented by
later artifacts such as tapestries from the Islamic period in the seventh
century A.D.

Guests in the more private quarters of the residence today are
quick to note such architectural features as a double reception hall, spi-
ral staircase, and a magnificent barrel-vaulted ceiling upstairs. Delicate
plasterwork, especially the ribs of fruit, flower, and oak-leaf appliqué,
abounds. The Beale House's small sitting room, where this plaster ornamentation is particularly intricate, is considered one of the most beautiful rooms in Washington. Egyptian ambassadors also have added rugs,
tapestries, and table pieces, frequently on loan from the Egyptian Museum and the Museum of Islamic Art in Cairo.

*Because of its curvilinear
facade outside and a
museum of Egyptian
antiquities within, the
Egyptian ambassador's
residence has become a
popular curiosity on the
diplomatic circuit.*

39

AS FLAMES LICKED 25 FEET THROUGH THE FROSTY
February air of 1961 and firefighters' hoses turned the magnificent
French embassy into an ice palace, Ambassador Hervé Alphand and
his wife changed from the formal attire they had worn to a dinner at the
Peruvian embassy—Nicole Alphand from a pale green evening dress
to a pragmatic woolen number—and calmly walked to safety.

Fire damage to the brick and gray stone Norman mansion,
which had started in the building's self-service elevator, was confined
to the tin and slate pitched roof and to servants' quarters, but the
pumpers' flood of water saturated Oriental carpets and empire sofas
and ruined wood paneling shipped over from Versailles. At midnight,
someone inquired of Madame Alphand if she and the ambassador
would spend the night there. "But of course," she exclaimed, as maids
skittered upstairs to make up their bed. Even by the standard of Washington's acknowledged "most embassy-like" residence, which had seen
grand banquets, benefit soirees, ambassadorial welcomes and farewells,
and Bastille Day bashes, the evening had been unforgettable.

The French bought the estate in Kalorama Heights (named for
a showplace of the early 1800s that overlooked the city there) for
$400,000 in 1936 from John Hays Hammond. The embassy is still said
to be the largest in the grand Sheridan-Kalorama area. It was the first
France had owned, rather than rented, and the republic got it lock,
stock, and barrelful of Hammond's elegant, if eclectic, furnishings,
which he had assembled the world over during a colorful career as a
mining engineer. Having made his first fortune in the gold fields and
railroad boardrooms of California, John Hays Hammond made a second in the diamond fields of the African Transvaal (where he led a re-
form movement, found himself in prison and sentenced to death, and
bought his way to freedom after paying a $125,000 fine), and yet a third
evaluating property around the world for wealthy investors.

Hammond and his wife, Natalie, moved to Washington in 1909;
they were close friends of President William Howard Taft (Hammond
had also been a pallbearer at the funeral of Grover Cleveland), and was
named by Taft as representative to the 1911 coronation of Britain's King
George V and to several international commissions. In 1917 they purchased the four-acre Kalorama estate, which William W. Lawrence—
who had made a fortune in paint and "white lead" (the now-discred-
ited pigment) had built in the style of the Vanderbilts seven years
before. When they were at home, the Hammonds entertained lavishly,
while raising three children. One—Harris Hammond—became a
noted inventor of devices for the piano and organ. After Natalie Hammond died of sleeping sickness in 1931, Hammond divided his time between homes in Massachusetts and Florida. The 34-room, three-story
mansion, with one of Washington's most spectacular views of Rock
Creek Park and the Taft Bridge, stood empty. The French republic
bought it one month before the 81-year-old Hammond died, moving
Ambassador and Madame André de Laboulaye's residence from 16th
Street on Washington's first Embassy Row. That mansion became a
rooming house.

RESIDENCE OF THE
AMBASSADOR OF FRANCE
Hammond House
2221 Kalorama Avenue, Northwest
J. Henri de Sibour, Architect
1910

*Seventeenth-century
paintings by Noël
Coypel in the French
ambassador's formal
dining room were
originally executed to
decorate the bedroom
of Louis XIV at the
Tuileries in Paris.*

On February 8, 1936, the de Laboulayes opened the old Hammond manor to guests for the first time in years. Invitees were dazzled by the home's great foyer, gigantic stone fireplace, heavy oak- or ivory-paneled walls, Gobelin tapestries, blue-velvet draperies, flagstone terraces, and formal gardens. And, of course, by the view. Some of the embassy's furnishings were Hammond hand-me-downs; others were selected by Madame de Laboulaye from the Garde-Meuble, the French national storehouse.

Just before World War II, the embassy's neighbors fretted that the adjacent vacant lot, on which "for sale" signs had been prominent, might fall to an apartment developer and that some unsightly high-rise might cut off both the air and the view. The French banished their fears by buying it themselves. "I'm going to clear those trees," announced Ambassador Gaston Henry-Haye, "all but a fringe of them, and extend the lawn. The house has always been too large for the setting."

But Henry-Haye was Vichy French, and Secretary of State Cordell Hull unceremoniously sent him packing in 1942, before many trees could fall. The estate was left empty, watched over by the Swiss legation. When Charles de Gaulle set up his provisional government in Paris in late 1944, he sent his minister of information, Henri Bonnet, to Washington as ambassador. Bonnet reopened the old Hammond house and bustled about seeking forgiveness for France's staggering war debt. Hellé Bonnet was one of Washington's most renowned hostesses. According to Hope Miller's *Embassy Row,* Madame Bonnet found her legendary parties "a pleasant enough way, I hope, to entertain a mob and keep everybody happy."

In 1957, when Hervé Alphand first presented his card, his first wife, Claude, set about lightening the decor. Francs loosened by the visit of President René Coty enabled the Alphands to plaster the former heavy oak-paneled entrance hall in cream, replace gloomy tapestries with brilliant Matisse and Vuillard paintings, and fill the house with fresh and artificial flowers. All of this was done for almost a song, which was appropriate, as social columnist Dorothy McCardle marveled, "since Claude Alphand is a noted chanteuse" who had sung in New York supper clubs while her husband fought in the French Resistance. Claude Alphand divorced her husband, in part, society columnists reported, because she could not stand the social life. Nicole, the new Madame Alphand, who was one of First Lady Jacqueline Kennedy's fastest friends, adored it.

In the comparatively serene years that have followed those times, the mansion has slipped into unassuming grandeur. The staff did scurry to make arrangements for General de Gaulle's visit in 1963 for the funeral of John F. Kennedy and, in 1981 and 1984, when President François Mitterrand made visits—the former for the Bicentennial of the Battle of Yorktown in Virginia. Otherwise, the embassy pace has been smooth and steady. But even today, when a fifth-generation descendant of the Marquis de Lafayette or a patron of the Red Cross ball or a European Community envoy comes to call, the old Hammond house again becomes the stuff of many rich tales.

The French ambassador's home, a Kalorama Heights landmark, has seen some of Washington's most elegant and sought-after parties and even some intrigue during the Vichy period.

RESIDENCE AND STAFF
OFFICES OF THE
AMBASSADOR OF GREECE

Jennings House

2221 Massachusetts Avenue, Northwest

George Oakley Totten, Jr., Architect

1906

THERE WAS SOMETHING ABOUT WASHINGTON—proximity to power, in no small measure—that was a magnet for men who made millions in mining. John Hays Hammond, W. W. Lawrence, and Tom Walsh all built monumental homes in Washington in the early years of this century. And so did Hennen Jennings, a Kentucky-born, Harvard-educated engineer and pal of Hammond's, who joined the millionaires' club by consulting to British gold-mining interests in South Africa and Venezuela. His house at Sheridan Circle years later became an embassy (Greece), as did those of Hammond (France), Lawrence (Portugal), and Walsh (Indonesia). Jennings commissioned George Oakley Totten, Jr., to design the house. Totten would become a preferred architect of wealthy Washingtonians and designed several other residences around Sheridan Circle (one of which, a couple of doors up the avenue, is also owned and used by the Greeks).

Sheridan Circle had been close to the outer reaches of Massachusetts Avenue until it was extended to Observatory Circle in the 1870s. It was a fancy, almost-suburban address for Hennen and Mary Jennings, and they entertained with verve and splendor. Mary, herself a mining magnate's daughter who had seen the arrival of the Pony Express near her home in California, would, with Hennen, live through the Boer War in South Africa, taste Victorian society in London, and make the social scene in New York. She was also a renowned philanthropist—earning the French Médaille de Reconnaissance for her work on behalf of the American branch of the Fatherless Children of France—and a tireless worker for the Washington Home for the Incurables. After her husband's death in 1920, Mary Jennings remained in the house until she rented it to the Greek government in 1935. Two years later a wealthy Greek-American business executive, William Helis, bought it and donated it to his native country.

Washington Daily News reporter George Abell was on hand for the house's regal housewarming as the Greek legation:

Everybody came crowding to the new legation . . . to drink champagne and Scotch, to gossip and to marvel. There might have been a jam except that the house is so huge.

"Wonderful," enthused the guests.

"This coffee ice cream is the best I've ever tasted."

"How do they do it?" whispered an Ambassador to a colleague.

"Everywhere—from the rose-colored drawing room to a cozy little corner, full of cigaret smoke and syphons, near the buffet—rose a clamor of praise."

The "beautiful, the bizarre, the banal" were on hand, Abell continued. "Adolf Hitler's special representative, tall, blond Herbert Scholtz, and his handsome wife, arrived at the same time. Bald and benevolent Dr. Ernst Meyer [German] first secretary, came in whistling 'Dei Wacht am Rhein' and swinging a malacca walking stick."

Three years later, the Greek ambassador, Demetrios Sicilianos, spoke about the house—and Greek cooking—with *Washington Times-Herald* reporter Carol Frink. "It always seems strange to me that when this house was built, some 30 years ago or so, there was no possible way

of foretelling that it would ever be used as a Greek legation. Yet the architecture, inside and out, is in the best Greek tradition. Even the detail is Greek — the drawing room and dining room are Corinthian, and the library is Ionic."

In the 1980s, after almost eight decades of high life, the building showed its wrinkles, and Ambassador George Papoulias and his wife, Emily, redecorated and brightened the mansion. Decorators Carol and Climis Lascaris found brooding mahogany paneling and heavy curtains in adjacent second-floor salons and ordered both rooms painted egg-shell white and opened to the sun. The ambassador's successor, Christos Zacharakis, an avid collector, uses the two salons to display items from his own personal collections, including artifacts from Greek archeological digs and a display of Greek "worry beads" in amber, jade, and a dozen other materials, used to bring luck or, just as often, to occupy hands.

The top two floors of the embassy are devoted to living and guest quarters for the ambassador and his family, who can look out on Embassy Row and down on the oversized flag of the Hellenic Republic, fluttering from a staff that is itself wrapped, barber-pole fashion, in the light blue and white colors of this romantic nation.

The Greek embassy's principal building is a Classical Revival structure anchoring Sheridan Circle. Greek-inspired touches adorn the building inside and out.

45

╤╥╤

CHANCERY OF INDIA

Depew House

2107 Q Street, Northwest

Chase & Ames, Architects

═══ *1901* ═══

No figure better symbol-
izes the heroism and the
heartache of the Indian
people than Mohandas
Karamchand Gandhi.
A statue of the
Mahatma sits outside
the ambassador's office.

IT WAS IN THE 2100 BLOCK OF Q STREET IN 1901
that prominent Washington physician T. Morris Murray and his wife,
Eleanor, had built an imposing granite and limestone house that would
one day become the Chancery of India. It later passed through several
families, including that of Undersecretary of the Treasury Ogden L. Mills,
but was best known as the home of the widow of the venerable U.S. Senator Chauncey Depew. May Palmer Depew had bought the Q Street
home two years after the death of her well-known husband, whom the
New York Times called "the most eminent elder citizen of New York City."
(A humorist and gifted orator, Depew had amassed a fortune as president and later chairman of the New York Central Railroad Company before serving in the U.S. Senate.) Like her husband, May Depew was a
lawyer and a skilled public speaker, much in demand on the philanthropic
circuit. When she died in 1940, her real estate holdings, including the
Washington house, went to her cousin, Mrs. Charles C. Glover, who had
a fabulous Washington estate of her own. (Like the Depew property, the
Glover grounds would one day see an embassy.) Mrs. Glover leased the
Q Street house to a variety of tenants, including the British Purchase
Agency and a couple who briefly turned it into the "Texas Guest House."

The Indian government bought the house in 1946 and connected
it to another building to create a chancery. India maintains a separate
center on Massachusetts Avenue where, among other events, Independence Day, August 15, and the birthday of Mahatma Gandhi, October
2, are celebrated.

CALL IT WHAT YOU WILL—"A FABULOUS ECLECTIC pile" (*Washington Post* architecture critic Benjamin Forgey in 1982); "very good, very rich, very ugly" (a guest at a lavish party about 1908, quoted by Forgey); or "a grand opera palace" (Elizabeth Ford in the *Washington Times-Herald* in 1953)—Tom Walsh's monument to overnight prosperity was the place to be seen in Washington in the first decade of this century.

An Irish immigrant millwright's apprentice who went west to join his brother in Colorado in the 1870s, Walsh built bridges in the town of Golden and, like thousands of other men, soon caught "gold fever." But unlike most of the others, Walsh more than struck it rich 8,000 feet up in the Rockies; he discovered a vein near Ouray, Colorado, so inexhaustible that he finally sold his Camp Bird mine in 1902 for $3.1 million, plus one-fourth share of future gold proceeds until they reached $2 million (which they soon did) and $100,000 worth of stock. Tom Walsh and his wife, Carrie, had more than a little money with which to enjoy the good life.

An interesting twist on the sale of the mine is that it was bought by a consulting engineer, John Hays Hammond, who also would later move into a grand Washington home that would become an ambassador's residence (see page 41). In his description of the negotiations over Camp Bird in his 1935 autobiography, Hammond quotes Walsh this way: "'I've already made several millions out of the mine, but I don't want to be tied up any longer. I've been in these mountains for many years. My children are growing up. I want them to have an education and some social life. . . .'" Hammond further observed that Walsh had aspired to social position "and attained it. . . . He died a wealthy man."

Appointed one of the American commissioners to the Paris Exposition of 1899, Walsh, according to a U.S. Commission of Fine Arts retrospective, converted a Seine River steamer into a "floating palace" on which a $40,000 dinner party was given for "distinguished men." Then the Walshes chartered their own train of five parlor cars, "fitted it with silk and decorations which he had used upon his steamer and commenced a tour of France and Belgium," picking up pointers along the way on how to build a grandiose estate.

In Ostend, Walsh met Belgian King Leopold II, who was interested in prying loose some of Walsh's millions for investment in the Congo; the king promised to stop and see Tom and Carrie in Washington en route to the St. Louis exposition of 1903. That posed a problem. The Walshes, who had moved to the nation's capital about 1897, owned a fine but hardly kingly home on Phelps Place, and the mining mogul was determined to have a showplace ready for His Majesty's visit. He bought 26,000 square feet of property on newly fashionable Massachusetts Avenue and commissioned Danish-born New York architect Henry Andersen to build, literally, a palace fit for a king. After spending more than $835,000 for the 60-room building and another $2.1 million for Persian rugs, French paintings, and other furnishings, in 1903 Tom and Carrie Walsh and their children, Evalyn and Vinson, moved into their palace. Critic Forgey described it as "a veritable pastry of or-

*Following page:
Ionic columns and
demonlike statues from
Bali frame the doorway
on the undulating
Massachusetts Avenue
facade of the Indonesian
embassy. The statues
are said to ward off evil.*

nament culled with skillful abandon from the Beaux Arts book of historical styles."

Affording it was not a problem. "Each morning, we Walshes arose richer than we had gone to bed," Evalyn would later write in her autobiography, *Father Struck It Rich.*

The house has a distinctive entryway rising three stories to a stained-glass, domed ceiling with a Y-shaped central staircase reminiscent of an ocean liner's, eight fireplaces, a ballroom and theater (for little "Vin," who played at acting), and bathtubs that, according to a *Washington Star* article in 1957, are "small swimming pools." The dining room is a replica of King Leopold's.

The king never made it to Washington, but his nephew, King Albert, and Queen Elizabeth did in 1919, nine years after Tom Walsh's death. Just as the Belgian royalty was arriving, President Woodrow Wilson suffered a stroke, and the White House was taken out of the entertainment loop. Mrs. Walsh volunteered her mansion for the state dinner, yielding the host's role to Vice President and Mrs. Thomas Riley Marshall. For the occasion, everything possible was Walsh gold, from the chrysanthemums and candelabra to the table service forged from Camp Bird ore.

Tom Walsh had got in his share of entertaining before he died. Even when he and Carrie dined alone, their organist, Dr. Harry Wheaton Howard of St. Aloysius Church, on yearly retainer, serenaded on the house's magnificent baroque organ. In *Father Struck It Rich,* Evalyn Walsh McLean recalled poking holes in a canvas screen that looked into a dining room and joining her brother, Vinson, in bombing her father's guests, including President William Howard Taft, with projectiles from a bean shooter. At a ball and cotillion soon after the house was opened in 1903, the Walshes welcomed Alice Roosevelt, daughter of President Theodore Roosevelt. Evalyn, deemed too young at 17, was not invited and pouted in her room. According to Helena McCartha, the *Evening Star*'s society editor, favors included lace fans with tortoiseshell handles for the girls and gold (not gold-colored) pencils for the men. "Poke bonnets and peasant headgear, cuff and handkerchief boxes, handbags and purses were other pretty and useful gifts," she reported. At another bash, 325 guests consumed 480 quarts of champagne, 288 fifths of scotch, 40 gallons of beer, and 36 bottles of liqueur. "It really is a palace that expresses dreams my father and mother had when they were poor in Colorado," she wrote in *Father Struck It Rich.* "This should not give rise to any notion they were sadly 'nouveau' as that term is used to label people outside of society trying to get in. We were in; make no mistake about it. . . ." Recalling the heydays of the mansion, she added, "How the money went!"

In 1905 Vinson was killed, and Evalyn badly injured, when Vin drove Evalyn's Mercedes off a bridge in Newport, R.I. A bathroom at "2020"—the Walshes' unpretentious name for their home—was turned into an operating room for Evalyn's hip surgery; she would wear a silver plate in her hip for the rest of her life. She also developed a morphine habit and wrote in her book about walking the cavernous house, night after night, loving this grand home even more.

In 1908 Evalyn and Edward Beale McLean, whose father owned the *Washington Post* and the *Cincinnati Enquirer,* eloped, but they were certainly not disinherited. After the death of Edward's father, they were living in their own urban paradise, the "Friendship" estate (site of today's McLean Gardens apartments) on Wisconsin Avenue, where their breakfasts on New Year's Day, Easter, and Thanksgiving became Washington traditions. They continued to drop in for soirees at their mother's mansion. Evalyn still kept many of her sables and silks in a top-floor room the size of a dress shop, and it was there in 1911 that the McLeans arranged to buy the Hope Diamond.

Inside the Walsh mansion, Evalyn's mother always busied herself with charitable endeavors. During World War I, she and her friends gathered up old clothes, turned the oak dining room into a sewing parlor, and fashioned garments for Belgian refugees. Once a week, she threw the house open to members of the service for music and dancing. The events became so popular that she had to issue admission cards to the "2020 Dancing Class."

The public-service tradition continued after Carrie Walsh's death in 1932. After standing empty for three years, the mansion was rented to the U.S. Resettlement Administration, whose mission was to provide suburban bungalows for city slum dwellers. Bureaucrats were observed having a fine time lunching on the grand staircase, typing letters in Mrs. Walsh's former boudoir, riding the gilded elevator, yanking on the servants' bell-cords, and dictating memos in front of the tapestried walls (wisely covered with cellophane to minimize staining). In 1937 the relocators moved out, their director admitting that placing a New Deal agency in such swanky quarters was unseemly and becoming a political millstone. More civil servants, from the U.S. Rural Electrification Administration, moved in for a time, but then the house fell empty again.

In 1940 there were press reports that the Walsh mansion would "go commercial," but instead Evalyn McLean and her mother's other trustees turned it over, rent free for 10 years, to the District of Columbia chapter of the Red Cross. In the house during World War II, Red Cross workers wrapped bandages—at the rate of 100,000 a month. At the time the lease expired in 1950, the Red Cross was using it as a center for educational services, and the Washington Workshop gave classes in sculpture, dancing, and art in the ballroom and other fourth-floor quarters.

The Republic of Indonesia, the nation of many islands—once called the Dutch East Indies—had won its independence in 1949 and

Evalyn Walsh McLean was a fancier of jewelry. A photograph from an *Evening Star* of the period shows her with a five-inch-high gold choker studded with diamonds. And the idea of owning the world's largest diamond intrigued her. The 44 ½-carat Hope Diamond was acquired from Cartier Frères of Paris for $154,000 ($40,000 down, the rest in three installments over three years). The *New York Times* reported that it would be worn by Evalyn McLean "as a head ornament arranged in a bandeau, the large stone being placed immediately in front with other diamonds of lesser size." Evalyn actually pawned the diamond a couple of times before selling it, in 1940, to New York jeweler Harry Winston, who donated it to the Smithsonian Institution.

Evalyn McLean would later insist the famous "curse" of the Hope Diamond had passed her by, but she did suffer a string of tragedies. In 1919 her son Vinson—the "hundred-million-dollar baby" who had slept in a crib made of gold, the gift of King Leopold—ran into traffic and was killed by a car. She and Edward were separated in 1930 and, three years later, he was declared insane, hospitalized, and died in 1941. "At intervals I get reports from a Maryland hospital concerning a patient there who has morbid preoccupations and lives in a state of mental exile," Evalyn wrote, "shut off even from himself. If he is addressed by his right name he grows excited and swears he is not McLean." Evalyn, who moved back to "2020," died in 1947.

was looking for suitable embassy quarters. In 1951 the Indonesians bought the Walsh mansion from Carrie Walsh's estate for $335,000, half a million dollars less (not even counting inflation) than Thomas Walsh had spent to build it 48 years earlier.

The Indonesians did not revive the mansion's elbow-bending party tradition; as Muslims, most Indonesians do not drink alcohol. But they did spend eight months and $75,000 to eradicate most of the vestiges of the palace's federal and institutional occupancy, replacing stained-glass panes in the entrance-hall ceiling, removing the termite-infested wooden floor in the basement and installing one of concrete, restoring Italian master paintings that had been damaged, stitching worn tapestries, and celebrating the Walshes' love of gold motifs where possible. At the embassy's opening reception in 1952, at which Ambassador Ali Sastroamidjojo presided, the 500 guests marveled at the gold brocade tapestry in the music room—and at Madame Sastroamidjojo's matching gold lace jacket.

Four years later, the *Washington Star*'s Selwa Roosevelt visited and found that "of the elaborate furnishings from the Walsh era nothing remains but a tiny white piano which once made happy music in the ballroom on the top floor. Now the piano is in the basement, looking a bit forlorn, with its keys discolored." In 1981 Sarah Booth Conroy toured the Indonesians' "warren of offices" and noted, "The house looks like a magnificent grande dame sent out to earn a living in a job to which her past life had not accustomed her."

The Indonesians added an exotic touch to the mansion with the installation of a *gamelan,* a 100-year-old collection of musical, chiefly percussion, instruments enjoyed by area students, embassy personnel, and guests at receptions, incorrectly described by the *Star* as "a pantry full of copper pots and pans." Visitors to those receptions still delight in hearing rumors that Tom Walsh had hidden a huge gold nugget in the house. One tale has it that the Indonesians, when they took over, found the treasure amid the flagstones of the front walkway (the Resettlement Administration workers and Red Cross volunteers somehow having stepped on it thousands of times without finding it).

But the legend is not apocryphal. In 1953 a Seton Hall professor who was a student of mining history—and of Thomas Walsh in particular—discovered a 12-by-15-inch slab of gold ore in the facing supporting the house's piazza. Lest Washingtonians descend with picks and jackhammers, he quickly pointed out that it takes a ton of such ore to yield $100 and that the artifact had no doubt been Tom Walsh's symbolic souvenir.

In 1982 the Indonesian government built a $1.3 million addition to the mansion—set back from Massachusetts Avenue as if in deference to the stately old building—which was designed by Architects Collaborative of Cambridge, Massachusetts. Several chancery functions moved there, with the grandest parts of the Walsh house thus made available for entertaining. Guests still stream through the door, passing under the Indonesian coat of arms symbolizing the nation's 1,300 islands. The motto upon it reads: "Unity through Diversity."

The Walshes' Louis XIV drawing room now holds the instruments of a traditional Indonesian gamelin orchestra, which once belonged to the Sultan of Jogjakhara, a royal court in Java.

51

RESIDENCE OF THE
AMBASSADOR OF ITALY

Villa Firenze

2800 Albemarle Street, Northwest

Russell Kluge, Architect

1927

*A majolica vase and
statue of a saint
rest atop a Louis XIV
table at the foot of
Villa Firenze's reception
room staircase.
Following pages:
The onetime home of
Colonel and Mrs.
Robert Guggenheim
has surprisingly
informal spaces such as
this enclosed sunroom.*

IF ANYONE WAS UNHAPPY TO LEARN THAT THE GOVernment of Italy had purchased Villa Firenze with the idea of turning its 59-room manor house into a residence for its ambassador in 1976, it was the tax-collection office of the District of Columbia, for the property had carried the sixth-highest tax assessment in the city. The purchase price was $4,335,000.

Firenze's gray Tudor mansion, made of brick, wood, stucco, and fieldstone—the stone quarried on the estate—was built in 1925 by Blanche Estabrook Roebling O'Brien, widow of a member of the firm that built the Brooklyn Bridge. Blanche O'Brien had a 60-foot-long swimming pool built first; she and her friends picnicked around it as the manor house rose and later twirled upon the wooden dance floor that covered the pool.

In the 1930s Blanche O'Brien leased the estate to the government of Hungary, which turned it into a popular diplomatic gathering place. In 1941 it was sold to Colonel Robert Guggenheim (a Silver Star veteran of World War I) and his wife, Rebecca "Polly" Guggenheim, who had been residing on their oceangoing yacht, *Firenze,* on the Potomac River when the U.S. Navy requested it for possible wartime service. Recalling another Tudor home in which he grew up—also named Firenze after his mother, Florence (*Firenze* in Italian)—Guggenheim, heir to the family copper fortune, promptly christened his new estate Firenze.

Colonel Guggenheim would briefly serve as President Eisenhower's ambassador to Portugal. After the colonel's death in 1959, Polly and her second husband, John Logan, lived in the house. Logan had founded a national association of food chains and had expanded its operations overseas. He was also the longtime chairman of Washington's Cherry Blossom Festival Ball. The Logans used Firenze for numerous community functions, often as a setting for the charitable sale of art. Polly also used the airy manor to show off her world-class collection of glass. When the sale to the Italian government was announced and the family was preparing to move furnishings to a winter home on St. Croix and to a new estate on S Street, N.W., Polly Logan told the *Washington Post,* "We'll have to have a garage sale . . . a six-car garage sale. Won't that be fun?" When she left, she took stone lions that had stood beside the garden terrace. "[They] go everywhere with me," she said. "I'm born a Leo, and lions are my symbol."

At first, little about Villa Firenze or its grounds strike one as Italian. From the back of the house, rolling hills and woods, part of the city's Rock Creek Park, recall the Cotswold area of southwest England. The driveway off Albemarle Street passes the gardener's cottage, painting studio, and garage. A second drive, off Broad Branch Road, winds through a thick woods. The embassy's enormous oak front door and its long heavy wrought-iron bell pull seem more appropriate for a residence of Henry VIII. Inside, a spacious entryhall with a minstrel's gallery, added by the Guggenheims, is paneled in pickled oak. The hall includes a rotunda ceiling featuring signs of the zodiac in bas-relief. Off the hall is one of the most unusual rooms in the house: the diminutive library where original owner Blanche O'Brien had installed

17th-century wood paneling taken from the study of British architect Christopher Wren, recreating the original study's exact dimensions.

While the architecture is derivative of English models, the furnishings are unmistakenly Italian, with pieces dating from the Baroque era. A 15th-century painting on wood of the madonna and child from the school of Sandro Botticelli and a carved wood statue of Catherine of Alessandria, a 14th-century saint, share space in the entrance hall. Some fabrics were woven at the Fortuny factory in Venice; 18th-century gold-inlaid mirrors come from Naples; crystal chandeliers and sconces hail from Murano, while decorative jugs come from the Capodimonte factory near Naples.

Villa Firenze is perfectly suited for entertaining (it has one of the largest dining rooms of any private home in the city). While a president of the United States rarely attends strictly social functions in diplomatic residences, President Ronald Reagan did attend a Columbus Day lunch here during his first administration. And the residence has hosted numerous celebrities throughout the years, including, for an awards dinner in 1989, tenor Luciano Pavarotti, writer Umberto Eco, and actress Sophia Loren, who on previous visits also had used the four-room suite upstairs during the tenure of Ambassador and Mrs. Rinaldo Petrignani.

This 39-room villa once was called "Estabrook," after its first owner, Blanche Estabrook Roebling O'Brien, who had the 60-foot outdoor pool built first so friends could loll and watch construction.

56

RESIDENCE OF THE
AMBASSADOR OF THE
IVORY COAST

Livingston's Vale
5111 Broad Branch Road, Northwest

1927

WHEN "WASH" WILLIAMS, OWNER OF WASHINGTON'S biggest Schlitz beer distributorship, and his wife in 1947 inspected the house they had heard was for sale at 5111 Broad Branch Road, they found more of a home than they bargained for. The fortresslike house that peers down on Rock Creek Park was sealed shut with boards, its interior caked in layers of dust, but what lay under the grime proved irresistible.

This place, where a whimsical intruder had drawn "Kilroy was here" in the dust, had been the home of eccentric world traveler Lily Livingston, who had died two years earlier, leaving a million-dollar estate including a horse farm in Virginia and a $1,000 bequest for the care of Pee Wee, her fox terrier. Lily's husband, George, a wealthy former New York public official, had built Livingston's Vale in 1927 on a part of the estate of contractor T. Franklin Schneider, who had built several of the Henderson 16th Street mansions that later became embassies.

Both the Williams family and the government of the Ivory Coast, which purchased the house as an ambassador's residence in 1961, added modern touches and altered the interior: the Williamses, notably, installed one of the area's first television sets and a candy-striped soda fountain soon after they moved in. The former French colony, in addition to installing twin swimming pools outside, has given the interior touches of the Ivory Coast through displays of various artifacts.

George and Lily Livingston had this mahogany staircase built into Livingston's Vale. It included a built-in organ and leads to a tiled veranda that had been pried from a Bavarian castle.

THE WINTER OF 1976–77 WAS A FRIGID, SNOWY ONE in Washington, literally putting on ice the construction of the new Japanese ambassador's residence, across the street from the National Presbyterian Church and NBC's television facilities. Plans for a grand opening on the April 29 national day had to be scrapped, and the celebration was held at the old neo-Georgian residence on Massachusetts Avenue. Japanese cherry trees had been planted in readiness at the new Nebraska Avenue location, a gleaming fountain and distinctive teahouse were in place, but, Ambassador Fumihiko Togo lamented, "mostly, the grounds are a sea of mud."

In 1972 the Japanese had purchased for $2 million the nearly eight-acre site bordering the Swedish embassy grounds from "Sittie" Parker, divorced wife of the board chairman of the Woodward & Lothrop department store. In the late 1800s the property had been the grounds for the prestigious Dumblane fox-hunting club on the Grassland estate of New Yorker S. S. Howland. The land was later part of the sprawling Glover estate owned by Riggs National Bank president and chairman Charles C. Glover. In addition to establishing Rock Creek, Potomac, and the National Zoological parks, Glover had also made possible the erection of American University buildings on his uptown land.

The Japanese razed the Parker house to make room for their new building, designed by American-born architect Masao Kinoshita of Watertown, Massachusetts. So hush-hush were negotiations, which had begun as early as 1970, that not even the U.S. Office of Protocol knew about them. The embassy staff had outgrown the old building, had been leasing extra office space at the Watergate apartment building, and needed the ambassador's Massachusetts Avenue quarters for chancery functions. One estimate placed construction costs of the new residence and its furnishings at $12 million.

The Parker place had boasted what *Star-News* writer Betty Beale called "fabulous trees," many 50 years old or more. "There are huge dogwood trees, a tremendous old Russian mulberry tree, an osage orange tree and any number of large old oaks," Beale wrote in 1972. "The big fruit of the osage orange is inedible but its very hard flexible wood once made it excellent bow material for the Indians. 'It's still considered the finest bow a sportsman can buy,' said Mrs. Parker."

Sittie Parker moved to a smaller house on Van Ness Street, where, Beale reported, "she will be able to watch the growth of whatever the Japanese create." Dozens of trees were indeed felled, but the Japanese imported others to replace them. As for the new house, an embassy official told the *Washington Post* that it would have the "feel and look" of a Japanese house. "In Japan, the traditional house is of wood and paper. That would not be practical in the Washington climate. So our new residence will be of stone and concrete." Its grand salon, longer than the White House ballroom and reminiscent, one observer said, of a huge hotel lobby, was designed to accommodate 500 for cocktails, its drawing room comfortable for 40 dinner guests.

Entertainment at Ambassador and Madame Togo's housewarm-

RESIDENCE OF THE
AMBASSADOR OF JAPAN
4000 Nebraska Avenue, Northwest
Masao Kinoshita, Architect
1977

The Japanese ambassador's residence contains spaces that are ultra-functional and others that are quietly contemplative. Eight landscape artists constructed the gardens and pond.

ing, when it was finally ready in November 1977, included a fashion show by couture designer Hanae Mori of New York, Tokyo, and Paris. Madame Togo herself wore a Mori creation that the designer said had taken 40 days to create. Supreme Court Justice Potter Stewart, who was in attendance, described one of the gowns as "straight from the 1920s—the flapper age, you know." Guests were somewhat startled at the size of the house at a time of increasing energy consciousness; two stories rise above ground, two more dip below. "When you're an embassy, you don't concern yourself with such mundane things," the *Post* quoted one visitor. Visitors admired the house's hand-blocked wallpaper and shoji screens.

A "must-see" at the old Massachusetts Avenue address had been the ambassador's garden and *ippakutei,* or teahouse, which had been prebuilt in Japan and reassembled here. It continued in use for a time after the Nebraska Avenue facility was in place because the new structure had not been properly consecrated by a tea master. The garden of the new residence, according to the *Post,* even included a pond ("man-made but with real carp") and a waterfall (which once flooded the teahouse). An embassy publication notes that "in style and in conception [it] resembles the early nineteenth century garden of the Kogetsu-tei of Sugata-an in Matsue, designed by the great feudal lord and tea master, Fumai Matsudaira." The garden's centerpiece is another teahouse, also imported from Tokyo, overlooking a pond, "purposely designed to be large, to give the illusion of the tea house floating upon it." A guide for visitors explains the elaborate tea ceremony:

The custom of drinking powdered tea in a tea ceremony was brought from China to Japan by a Buddhist monk, Eisai, toward the end of the 12th century. In the 16th century, the fundamentals of the tea ceremony were perfected by a Zen monk, Sen no Rikyu, who summarized its basic idea in four words: WA, KEI, SEI, and JAKU. WA is harmony, the harmony among people and with nature; KEI is respect, an expression of gratitude towards all things; SEI is purity; JAKU is tranquility of man and nature. Thus the spiritual foundation of Chanoya is derived from Zen Buddhism for which [the] essence of reality and beauty is simplicity.

While designed to evoke a contemplative Buddhist setting, the imperial-size residence, sprawling over 1.6 acres, has become the center of elaborate Kabuki plays, benefit balls, and displays of Japanese commerce and cultures—activities that now better represent a frenetic modern Japan.

The tea ceremony house was dedicated in 1960 to 100 years of Japanese-U.S. relations. Behind a partly concealed panel, the host makes ceremonial preparations as guests enjoy the serene view.

AROUND A COUPLE OF BENDS BEHIND AMERICAN
University, on the edge of Spring Valley, sits one of Washington's most
contemporary diplomatic residences—and most faithful architecturally
to the nation whose ambassador it serves. Designed by South Korea's
fabled postwar Space Group architect, Swoo-Guen Kim—master architect of the 1988 Olympic Games complex in Seoul—and executed
by Washington architect Jack Samperton, it has all the solemn trappings of an upper-class Yi Dynasty villa. However, its 18,000-square-
foot floor space, ceremonial entrance, large reception hall, several
wings, and central courtyard would dwarf such residences in that nation. Kim died in 1986, before the building officially opened on October 3 of that year, Korea's Foundation Day holiday, Kae Chun Chal.
More than 1,000 people attended the housewarming without crowding
the residence. A few days earlier, Ambassador and Madame Kyung-
Won Kim had hosted members of the Spring Valley Citizens' Association, whose fears about having an embassy in their midst had been
soothed by the quiet dignity of both the building and its occupants.

The ideal Korean home faces south, has hills or mountains to its
north, a water source to the south, and is surrounded by trees. The
sunny southern exposure, murmuring stream, and shade from the summer sun are optimum, and Kim and Samperton delivered on all but the
hills, which are humble in Spring Valley.

The house sits on grounds once owned by Robert Whittier Dudley, the Washington lawyer and executive who, with his wife, Argentina,
daughter of a former ambassador from the Dominican Republic, raised
six children and entertained spectacularly at Gatesley, their Tudor-style
home built by the ubiquitous W. C. and A. N. Miller Company, devel-
opers of Spring Valley. In 1978, in turn, Dudley—despairing, neighbors
say, of D.C. taxes and intrusions onto the property by inebriated American University students—sold the house and its land to the Koreans
and moved to Maryland. The Space Group kept the house vacant for
many years and finally demolished it.

While the $4 million ambassadorial dwelling has many of the el-
ements of a fragile Korean structure, with wood and stucco predomi-
nating, the architects hid the supporting steel beams and opted for copper roofing rather than traditional clay roof tiles. Samperton said Kim
chose copper for the roofing because the green patina that would ap-
pear as it aged would blend with the natural surroundings. Wooden
columns, beams, staircases, and buttresses proliferate, as do pagodas,
lanterns, and a pond reminiscent of home. Wisconsin pine lamination,
which came in thousands of pieces that had to be meticulously pieced
together as one might master a sophisticated Lincoln Log set, masks the
steel skeleton. The courtyard's small pond is square with a round island
in its midst, a configuration derived from the Oriental philosophy of the
balance of life—Yin (the square-shaped pond as earth) and Yang (the
round island as the sky). Simplicity is served in the paper-covered
changhoji doors in the grand passageway to the second-story grand
banquet room. More than 300 of the panels for windows and doors
were constructed in Korea and installed by Korean craftworkers. Tra-

RESIDENCE OF THE
AMBASSADOR OF KOREA
4801 Glenbrook Road, Northwest
Swoo-Guen Kim, Architect
1986

ditional Korean ricepaper screens were used in windows, creating translucent screens using up to 10 layers of the paper. Also from Korea are rugs, musical instruments, lanterns, sculptures, and paintings.

Only one cherished Korean tradition seems lacking, but of necessity, given the building's function: privacy. *Washington Post* critic Benjamin Forgey, in his review of the house in 1986, noted, "The flaw has become ever more apparent as the splendid deciduous trees in the front yard have shed their leaves." That aside, though, Forgey observed, guests were charmed by the residence's white panels and lanterns, which delivered "a sense of being in another place and time. It was for such moments especially that this house was designed."

ONE OF THE FIRST GOVERNMENTS IN THE 1960S
to take advantage of the opening of the old National Bureau of Standards grounds as a chancery preserve—located in uptown Washington overlooking Rock Creek Park—was the state of Kuwait. It commissioned Baltimore architect Van Fossen Schwab to design what the *Washington Star* called "the most unique embassy in Washington." It was certainly anything but the typical classicist mansion. Some critics described it as "Arabesque," others as the epitome of the wealthy nation's "progress and modernism." Still another called it "the Embassy-Palace of Kuwait."

Architect Schwab got the Kuwaiti commission after helping the nation, newly independent after years as a British protectorate, acquire land on Tilden Street from the Chevy Chase Land Company. He consulted with Kuwaitis both in Washington and in New York, where Ambassador Talat Al-Ghoussein was also Kuwait's envoy to the United Nations, but Schwab never visited the emirate before or after completing the project. Schwab recalls that the ambassador joked that he wanted to "walk to work," so the residence wing was not connected directly to the chancery. The diplomat also wanted the large central reception area to be an extension of his home, so it was cut off from the chancery as well.

"There were a lot of ups and downs" in the relationship, Schwab says, beginning with the tight $700,000 construction budget. "They were a new nation with a full head of steam. Before we were done, they went through seven different interior decorators."

Schwab recalled a problem he had with the project's model:

Once, we were working on the arches. We retained a sculptor to study the various lighting approaches and came up with a model made of plaster of paris. The Ambassador was in New York, so I wrapped the model in brown paper and very carefully took it up on the train. I got it through Pennsylvania Station and into and out of a cab to the Waldorf-Astoria. But when I went into the hotel through one of those revolving doors, someone came barreling through the other way and caught the package in the door. The model shattered into a thousand pieces. I took the brown-paper wrapping upstairs and opened it. Nobody laughed.

Schwab and interior designer Valerian Rybar of New York created two separate, beige-brick buildings trimmed in white, a single facade of two-story, precast concrete "Islamic arches" (centuries old in inspiration, the *Washington Post* said), connected by a glass-enclosed loggia. A huge metal and glass seal of Kuwait dominates one glass wall, while marble chips glitter in the exterior walls and metal grilles cover windows. Specially added were a swimming pool, inconspicuous air-conditioning slats, and parking facilities. Even diplomatic titles had a new-coined air. Where most embassies parade princes, naval attachés, and chargé d'affaires at official functions, the development-conscious Kuwaitis honored their "minister of electricity and water" at one of the first receptions.

Designer Rybar maintained "the mood of Middle East splendor," reporter Ruth Wagner noted, in his "first attempt at diplomatic decoration [which] should be a natural for him, since he was educated

CHANCERY AND RESIDENCE
OF THE AMBASSADOR
OF KUWAIT
2940 Tilden Street, Northwest
Van Fossen Schwab, Architect
1966

in Europe for a diplomatic career." Inside, visitors admired the Baccarat crystal chandeliers, purchased from a museum in India, which hang in the embassy's central hall; the leather paneling of walls and doors; and the walls of the central reception loggia—a mosaic of 27,000 carved pieces of walnut. On one wall, Madame Al-Ghoussein hung a Persian rug. Eighteen laborers, brought from Cairo, completed the installation in three months, hurrying to finish by January 18, 1966, in order to get back to Egypt for the feast of Ramadan. The building's lattice screening and much of the furniture were designed and carved by hand in Cairo and shipped to Washington in pieces. The Omayyad Room—dating to 1755—was removed from a palace in Damascus and reassembled here. One observer called the result the "Seduction Room," because of its low lighting and dark cedar paneling, low divans, and colorful pillows.

The Kuwaitis' sitting room borrows thematic Islamic arches from the exterior.

Opposite:
In a salon dubbed the "Seduction Room" by visitors who had seen too many Valentino movies, gold brocade lines the niches of the carved Arabesque paneling.

Although *Post* architecture critic Wolf Von Eckardt granted that the overall result was a "new bit of Arabic delight," he wondered if the "rich oil wells of that small Arab nation . . . might have wrought just a little more." Citing the "slight Thousand-and-One-Nights fakery," he wondered, "Why is the tile so pale and nondescript? And why, in Omar Khayyam's name, the mud-colored antique brick?"

"With such an embassy belonging to a country, however small (though it has a higher per capita income than ours)," wrote the *Washington Star* as the embassy prepared to open with a dinner for Vice President and Mrs. Hubert Humphrey, "Washington will watch with interest to see if Ambassador and Mrs. Al-Ghoussein play a leading role among diplomatic hosts in America." They and their successors have done so, and their national-day festivities in February have been marked by exuberant nonalcoholic toasts.

In no time, the embassy outgrew its space and added onto the reception area, Schwab says. "They became the biggest entertainers in town." The Kuwaitis also built a separate chancery elsewhere in town, keeping the Tilden Street structure as a residence and exhibition facility. Schwab voices regret "that as a result of terrorist activities [around the world], they had to put up a fence out front and a guardroom. It's not the greatest, aesthetically."

During the 1990–91 Persian Gulf War, in which Kuwait fought to rid itself of its Iraqi invaders, the embassy became a listening post and gathering place for the city's Kuwaiti nationals, who dubbed themselves the Kuwait Liberation Committee. Several students, brought to Washington for a summer program, remained in the embassy's care until Kuwait's liberation.

=◖◗=

CHANCERY AND RESIDENCE
OF THE AMBASSADOR
OF LITHUANIA

A Henderson House
2622 16th Street, Northwest
George Oakley Totten, Jr., Architect

= 1908 =

Delicate table settings,
figurines, and native
dolls fill the old
Lithuanian legation.
Many had gathered
dust in cold, closed-off
rooms during the
austere times before the
nation's liberation.

FOR 50 YEARS UNTIL THE CYCLONIC EVENTS OF 1990 and 1991, the largest piece of free Lithuania was a 17,000-square-foot plot of land on 16th Street in Washington, an ocean away from the tormented Baltic homeland. On the property sat the valiant "symbolic embassy," the Lithuanian legation, presided over by a persevering chargé d'affaires and the two or three staff members whose salaries were paid by Lithuanian-American supporters and the old republic's U.S. gold reserves. These reserves had been frozen by the United States and pooled with those of the other subjugated Baltic states, Latvia and Estonia, by the Federal Reserve after the Soviet army marched into tiny, 959-square-mile Lithuania in June 1940 and installed a "People's Government" parliament at the point of a gun. Under first the Bolsheviks, then Hitler as his forces drove toward Leningrad, then the "liberating" Soviets again, hundreds of thousands of Lithuanians were shipped to gulags, and almost all of the nation's Jews were massacred.

Lithuania had been a proud medieval kingdom. The Vytis, a sword-wielding knight on a charger, carrying a shield with the double-cross (‡), believed to symbolize the union of a Lithuanian prince and his Polish bride, is still the national emblem, and the Lithuanian language is one of the oldest living tongues. But Lithuania has also endured the indignities of many intrusions, first by Russia's Peter the Great and later by Germany's Kaiser Wilhelm, and, worst of all, following 22 years of fragile independence after the Treaty of Versailles, by the Red Army on the heels of the duplicitous 1939 Molotov-Ribbentrop Pact.

The Lithuanian minister to Washington at the time, Povilas Zadeikis, refused the demand that he turn over his legation to Soviet control, and he held forth there for another 18 years. The Italianate house with its tower had been one of a dozen or so built for U.S. Senator and Mrs. John B. Henderson, who had attempted to create a regal 16th Street diplomatic neighborhood just after the turn of the century (see page 90). In the first 15 years following its completion in 1908, this mansion was rented off and on to individual envoys, but it frequently stood empty. Marc Peter, the Swiss minister to the United States, had occupied the house just before Mary Foote Henderson sold it to the government of Lithuania for $90,000 in 1924. She received $5,000 down and then refused to accept additional payments, despite many efforts by the Lithuanians to proffer them. Following her death in 1931, the estate and the Lithuanian government settled the balance.

Nine years later, when Lithuania was overrun by Red Army troops, the United States, with a handful of other nations, while gingerly avoiding full diplomatic recognition of legitimate Lithuania, refused to acknowledge the little nation's absorption into the Soviet Union. In the years that followed, Zadeikis was forced to work in heavy-hearted limbo. He and his successors had no nation to which to report and no way to visit or even correspond with their compatriots. Funds to keep up the aging house, with its leaking roof and weed-choked garden, including rue, a herb that figures in national folklore, were meager.

Still, once a year, on February 16, the legation would sponsor a

modest cocktail reception, attended mainly by Lithuanian Americans and a few members of diplomatic society, to mark the 1918 independence anniversary. Ironically, two of the guests who did show up at the legation's 20th-anniversary independence party in 1938 were Ambassador and Madame Alexander Troyanovsky of the Soviet embassy, who, a society correspondent reported, hobnobbed with the hosts and guests from Latvia and Estonia. This conviviality reigned a year before Joseph Stalin's connivance with Adolf Hitler would consign all three nations to Soviet domination.

The *Washington Star* described Chargé d'Affaires Stasys A. Backis, then 72, as a "sad-eyed man without a country." On this occasion, Backis turned to a map of his homeland, hanging in the darkened hallway outside his office, and pointed to Joniskelis, the town of his birth on the River Musa. "He has not been there for 40 years," wrote *Star* reporter John Sherwood, "and will never be able to return."

Somehow the mission held on. Stasys Lozoraitis, Jr., who arrived as chargé in Washington in 1987 after a 17-year stint as chief of the Lithuanian mission to the Vatican, recalls, "It was like crossing the desert, having to concentrate on survival, of where we had to go, and of having the determination to get there. We had this. We would never give up, never give up, even after receiving blow after blow. We were waiting for history to turn, since history is so full of surprises. Of course it did, but, candidly, we thought we were working for the next generation, or if not some point 20 years from now, maybe 50 years, maybe 100 years."

The mansion, which Lithuanian Americans paid to have minimally renovated in the 1980s, served as a symbol over the years, "a silent, beautiful lady," Lozoraitis says. Meanwhile Lozoraitis and his wife began to dress up the 31-room mansion, restoring a second-floor reception area with brocaded walls and Renaissance Revival details to its former glory and installing contemporary and folk art pieces. In the basement was found a 1939 canvas by painter Petras Kalpokas commemorating the signing of the Lithuanian declaration of independence in 1918, now placed prominently in the embassy's entrance hall.

Then, in 1990, what had been the improbable dream for "The Land of Northern Gold" (coined for the amber yielded from the Baltic Sea) happened with breathtaking speed. Lithuania, whose independence movement, Sajudis, had been above-board as early as 1988, was the first Baltic nation to declare its separation from the U.S.S.R., for which it suffered both Moscow's economic boycott and deadly provocations involving Soviet troops. Following the foiled Moscow coup of August 1991, Soviet President Mikhail Gorbachev announced that he was prepared to release the Balts from Soviet control. "What has happened to my country is one of history's miracles," Minister Lozoraitis said as he prepared to leave on a trip to the Holy See, where he was concurrently the Lithuanian representative. He left knowing that he would be bringing back credentials to President Bush that would change his rank to ambassador and the suddenly sunny legation into a full embassy.

It took some time for Mary Foote Henderson, denizen of 16th Street's Embassy Row, to get the Lithuanians to buy the Italianate house that bore some of the same brooding features of her own "castle."

FAMILIAR NAMES POP UP IN THE HISTORY OF THE
Grand Duchy of Luxembourg's Louis XV limestone and brick manor
on Massachusetts Avenue. The Kalorama Heights land on which it sits
was owned by Katherine Medill McCormick (see page 27). The property passed through one more owner before Alexander and Margaret
Gray Stewart bought it in 1908 and commissioned the prominent New
York architects Jules Henri de Sibour and Bruce Price to build a house.
De Sibour, a native of France and trained in Paris, was active in Washington, where he built the Chevy Chase Club, Howard University's Science Hall, and many residences, including two separate Kalorama Road
homes for W. W. Lawrence that became the residences of the ambassadors of France and Portugal. The construction cost of the Stewarts'
new four-story home was estimated at $92,000.

Alexander Stewart had been a congressman from Wisconsin
who made his fortune buying huge chunks of prime Midwest timber-
land. The sons of Scottish immigrants to New Brunswick, he and his
brother John immigrated to the United States and made their way to
bustling Milwaukee in the 1850s. From there, so the story goes, he
walked to Wausau, 170 miles as the crow flies, in the Wisconsin timber
country. The young men took jobs as millhands at $16 a month but
asked to be paid in lumber and shingles, which they saved and then
floated down the Mississippi River to St. Louis and sold at a handsome
price. The Stewarts soon managed, then owned, Wausau's largest lumber mill. Alexander ventured into politics, served three terms in the
House of Representatives, and stayed in Washington after leaving
Congress in 1900. After Stewart's death in 1912 from a fall while visiting a paper mill, his wife and three daughters, Helen, Margaret, and
Mary (and Helen and Margaret's husbands), in various turns, lived in
the house until 1937, when, according to a report of the U.S. Commission of Fine Arts, Mary left it vacant until she sold it in 1941 to H.R.H.
Charlotte, the grand duchess of Luxembourg, for $40,000, far less than
the $104,000 assessed value of the property. "The house is a handsome
one and would have been, later, an excellent site for an uptown hotel,"
society columnist Helen Essary commented. "The coat-of-arms of the
little principality is being cut in stone above the door."

The grand duchess did not live in the house, the commission report continues, "but spent her time in Montreal and London, where her
ministers in exile were located during the German occupation of her
country." Instead, the duchy, which had maintained a legation at the
Shoreham Hotel, moved those functions to the Massachusetts Avenue
house. The grand duchess's mother, Dowager Grand Duchess Maria
Anna, did live in the house. When Maria Anna moved to town in 1941,
the *Washington Times-Herald* noted, "Washington, which has grown a little blasé over visiting royalty, can sit up and take notice. . . . Because of
her advanced age—80 years—and because she is mourning for the
death of a member of her family, there will be no entertaining, either
formal or otherwise." The dowager grand duchess died a year later. In
September 1944 the Luxembourg legation was the first, and only, diplomatic establishment to celebrate openly the Allies' liberation of Axis-

RESIDENCE OF THE
AMBASSADOR
OF LUXEMBOURG

Stewart House
2200 Massachusetts Avenue, Northwest
J. Henri de Sibour and Bruce Price, Architects

1908

operated countries in Europe. Minister Hughes Le Gallais raised the red, white, and blue flag of his nation atop the balcony of the legation.

Luxembourg's legation received embassy status in 1955, and seven years later its government bought a rowhouse building in the block, at 2210 Massachusetts—formerly the Israeli chancery—for use as a chancery, then purchased the main house for $160,000 from the grand duchess and made it the ambassador's residence.

Washington Post columnist Dorothy McCardle dropped by and was overcome by "the sudden feeling that you have been transported into the ancestral home of the descendants of Marco Polo. All around you are reminders of Venice, hometown of the famous explorer and also of Madame Le Gallais. . . . You are surrounded by priceless scrolls, paintings, vases, sculpture and chests from the Orient, lands first opened up to Western eyes by Italy's most famous traveling man back in the thirteenth century."

*Behind an entrance
hall statue in the
Luxembourg
ambassador's home,
the stairway's carved
balustrade depicts
various flora and fauna.
Opposite:
Representative
Alexander Stewart
lived in this
mansion only four
years before
his accidental death.*

71

MEXICAN CULTURAL
INSTITUTE

MacVeagh House
2829 16th Street, Northwest
Nathan Wyeth, Architect

1911

*The music room of the
Mexican Cultural
Institute features an
organ and a chair in
the Louis XIII style.
Following pages:
The sweeping hallway
mural is a fresco by
Roberto Cueva del Rio.*

WASHINGTON SOCIETY WAS AGOG IN 1911 AS GEORGE A. Fuller Company laborers put the finishing touches on an imposing four-story, buff-brick mansion on 16th Street in what was becoming the city's newest enclave of fashionable residences and embassies. Part of the land had been purchased from Mary Foote Henderson, the redoubtable developer of Meridian Hill, by a trust appointed by the mansion's secret owner. Repeated inquiries to workmen and the building's designer, Nathan Wyeth of New York—who had recently completed a house for Hattie Sanger Pullman down the street (later to be the Imperial Russian embassy)—elicited no information on the owner of this magnificent new structure, and the gossip intensified.

Among several persons who wangled private tours was William Howard Taft's secretary of the treasury, Franklin MacVeagh. MacVeagh and his wife, Emily, lived in another famous Washington house, Marshall Field's former Pink Palace, a stone's throw away. The secretary, who had been schooled in law but made his fortune as a wholesale grocer in Chicago, also dabbled in architecture. On Christmas eve, according to legend, as the MacVeaghs strolled through the new house, completely furnished and tidy, MacVeagh complimented the "exquisite taste" of the mystery owner. "Well if you like it," Emily MacVeagh was said to have replied, "you may have it as a Christmas gift!" As the story goes, Emily MacVeagh had been the mystery owner all along.

Indeed, a Merry Christmas present was the $120,000 home, with its lavish music room emulating the one in the French royal palace at Fontainebleau, pipe organ and chimes, the largest dining room in the city, and 14-carat gold leaf on the walls of the drawing room. A 1925 *Washington Star* article described the worth of this gilt wallpaper as "almost equal to what an average man might produce in a lifetime." (A bubble-burster, columnist Evelyn Peyton Gordon, writing in the *Washington Daily News* after touring the mansion, would flatly declare 21 years later, "I want to add that the renowned gold-leaf on the drawing room walls was not removed by the Ambassador and sent to Mexico. Actually there was no gold-leaf. It was only paint—and very dirty.")

When the MacVeaghs moved in and toasted their new home, President Taft and his debutante daughter, Helen, were the guests of honor. So taxing was the electrical overload of the affair that the lights went out, and Mary Foote Henderson and others scurried to their homes to find candles.

After a long illness, Emily MacVeagh died in 1916. Her husband moved out of the 26-room house and returned to Chicago, saying he could not bear to live in a place that so reminded him of his beloved Emily. He leased it to Assistant Secretary of State Breckinridge Long, who put the home at the disposal of Lord Balfour, head of the British mission, and then King Albert and Queen Elizabeth of Belgium during their visit in 1919. In 1921 MacVeagh sold the residence and many of its furnishings to the government of Mexico for $330,000. He asked two concessions of the Mexicans—that they make no significant alterations during his lifetime, and that his favorite servant be given lifetime employment.

72

Both were granted, if one does not count a chancery wing, garage, and portico entrance, which the Mexicans immediately added. They also filled the house with Mexican art, including Aztec sculpture. After MacVeagh's death, at age 97 in 1934, Ambassador Manuel Tellez—later dean of the city's diplomatic corps—continued the "Mexicanization" of the home, dispersing some of the MacVeagh furnishings and turning parts of the house into a model Mexican salon. Native flowers, cacti, and other plants were added to the roof garden; colorful Mayan murals were painted; and strolling guitarists became a fixture at receptions. A second-floor mural, part of a series by Cuevo Del Rio that rise along a grand staircase from the first floor to the third, depicts the solidarity of Western Hemisphere nations. The gold, or gold-colored, wallcovering disappeared. In 1941 the embassy covered the walls of the solarium with Talavera tiles from the city of Puebla, which depict two great Mexican volcanoes as well as the coats of arms of the nation and its 29 states, and also added a fountain.

After another renovation in 1946, much Mexican silver was brought into the house, including tableware and small decorative objects, and the "Mexicanization" was complete.

One of the most memorable affairs in the building, in 1957, feted the celebrated Mexican comedian Cantinflas. After the ambassador moved out in the late 1980s, the house became the Mexican Cultural Institute, which offers a wide range of programs and art exhibitions throughout the year.

The MacVeaghs entertained the capital's glitterati in the music room of the house that had been Emily MacVeagh's surprise Christmas gift to her husband. When she died, Franklin moved out.

RESIDENCE OF THE
AMBASSADOR OF THE
NETHERLANDS

Owsley House
2347 S Street, Northwest
Ward Brown, Architect

1929

THE HOME OF THE DUTCH AMBASSADOR PROVIDES
yet another example of a grand dwelling constructed for an out-of-town
tycoon. San Francisco–born architect Ward Brown, who designed or
restored dozens of homes in Alexandria and Georgetown, created this
house for Chicago "traction baron" Louis Septimus Owsley. President
of his own small streetcar and elevated trolley lines, Owsley was an
officer in a slew of other transit companies owned by Charles Tyson
Yerkes, who built and controlled street and "el" lines on Chicago's north
and west sides at the turn of the century. When Yerkes left Chicago to
go to London to develop that city's subway system, Owsley and his family moved to Washington. Just why is unclear; there is no record of his
business activities here, and he left no discernible historical footprint.

His classic square, four-story house was built on compact
grounds in 1929 at a cost of $90,000 by Wilmer Bolling, brother of the
second Mrs. Woodrow Wilson and one of many contractors and investors of the period who speculated in what became prime real estate.
It sits across S Street from the house where President Wilson retired
and which is now a property of the National Trust for Historic Preservation. "We moved 19 times before I was 16 years old," recalls Bolling's
son, Sterling. "He'd build a house, and we'd live in it for a while, and
then someone would come along and offer to buy it at fantastic prices.
So we'd go back to an apartment like the St. Regis while he built another place. Of course, back then there was open land to be bought
right in the city."

A peek past the
ornamented pediment
into the living room of
the Dutch ambassador's
home reveals a 17th-
century portrait of
stadholder Willem II
by Gerard Honthorst.
Following page:
The residence's trade-
mark tulips are a
perennial attraction.

In 1929 the Architects' Advisory Council report commended Brown's design of the Owsley House—with its nine master bedrooms and seven servants' bedrooms among 30 rooms—as one that "meets exceptionally well the standards which should be maintained for private buildings in the National Capital." Classical Revival on the outside, it features Adamesque details inside, inspired by the work of the Adam brothers in Scotland and England in the late 18th century. "Particularly interesting are the use of decorative urns and the inclusion of curvilinear pediments over the doorways in the dining and living rooms." The balustrade of the central staircase, which divides at a landing, is copied from Marie Antoinette's Petit Trianon at Versailles.

When Owsley retired to Wilton, Connecticut, in 1942, he sold the S Street house to the government of the Netherlands. Since the Netherlands acquired the mansion, ambassadors and their wives have decorated with 17th- and 18th-century Dutch and Flemish art, Dutch-crafted furniture, elaborate tapestries, and Holland's distinctive blue and white Delftware. From time to time the embassy has printed an elaborate floor plan, pinpointing each rare piece, crediting its creator and describing its origin.

Naturally the modest gardens always blaze to life during the spring tulip season. Or almost always. The March 1955 issue of *Diplomat* magazine reported, "Hansen, the gardener for Holland, hasn't recovered from the way the tulips stayed underground during the Springtime visit of Her Majesty, Queen Juliana, back in '52." The bulbs, inventively planted to form a welcoming "J," had been late arriving for planting because of a dockworkers' strike in New York. On another occasion in 1966 the flowers got several shots of hot water from a nervous staff when temperatures hovered around freezing the night before the tulip reception. Reported the *Washington Post*'s Judith Martin:

One diplomatic idea, which never quite materialized this year, was to bring varieties which are named after Washingtonians. There are countless varieties of tulips, so there's one named after just about everybody, and it's just a matter of selecting the right one.

State visits are particularly productive of tulip names—there's a Farah Diba one from the last Iranian visit, for instance—and there was a Queen Elizabeth (red, edged with yellow) among the lot at yesterday's party.

The only American doing vase duty was the Bing Crosby tulip (scarlet), although there was a Michigan bouquet (purple, white base) at the doorway.

Rain, freeze, Americana touch or not, however, the embassy's March tulip time is etched as a "can't miss" on the city's social calendar.

A fascinating footnote on Louis Owsley: Wealthy enough to build a palatial 30-room mansion in Washington in 1929, he reportedly died—divorced and almost penniless—in a nursing home in Connecticut in 1943. But in 1960, when Owsley's son learned that his father had left more than half a million dollars to his old prep school, Phillips Academy of Andover, Massachusetts, the son sued the academy and a New Haven bank, contending that Owsley was of unsound mind at his death because of severe brain damage suffered during a long illness. There is no available record as to whether the son won his case.

CHANCERY AND RESIDENCE
OF THE AMBASSADOR OF
PORTUGAL

W. W. Lawrence House

2125 Kalorama Road, Northwest

J. Henri de Sibour, Architect

1914

IT WAS NOT UNCOMMON IN THE HALCYON DAYS OF the private-club set in the early part of this century for the captains of industry to buy lots in Washington and put houses on them with the studied nonchalance of the Monopoly game's monocled tycoon. The same family name would often pop up in building permits, deeds, and tax records for several addresses. This was because still-verdant city land was available and cheap, industrial titans had the money to speculate, or they built homes for relatives as well as themselves. The W. W. Lawrence house that became the Portuguese ambassador's residence represented all three reasons.

"Billy" Lawrence was a Pittsburgh man who made his first fortune in the paint business, joining his father in starting a company that thrived making "Tiger Brand" paint and varnish and later was bought by Sherwin-Williams of Cleveland. Lawrence made his second killing in white lead, a principal (and, later generations would learn, deadly) element in his paint. He founded the Sterling White Lead Company in Pittsburgh, then became treasurer and later president of the bigger National Lead Company in New York. Lawrence and his wife, Jane, moved to Manhattan and became active in a long list of posh clubs.

Two of Lawrence's three sisters—Annie, a widow, and Mary, unmarried—lived in Washington in a rented house in what was known as Tuttle's Subdivision of Widow's Mite—now called Kalorama. In 1908 Lawrence began buying lots next door, and in 1910 he also opened a Washington outlet store for his paint at 1710 14th Street. That same year he commissioned prominent New York architect Jules Henri de Sibour to build a home for Annie and Mary on his Widow's Mite land. Billy Lawrence would use it only as an occasional place to hang his hat while in Washington. A year after Lawrence's death in 1916 at age 88, Annie and Mary Lawrence's Kalorama home was sold to mining magnate John Hays Hammond, whose heirs later sold it to France for a grand ambassadorial residence (see page 41).

In 1914 a second Lawrence home—also a de Sibour creation and the subject of this chapter—went up next door on Kalorama Road. This was an investment property; prominent Americans, including Secretary of Commerce Robert Lament and Assistant Secretary of the Treasury James Douglas, rented it. Eventually Annie Lawrence sold the house to Senator Gilbert Hitchcock of Nebraska, and in 1945 Hitchcock's widow, Martha, sold the house and part of the grounds to the republic of Portugal.

The Kalorama community in which both homes stand regally is at least 27 years older than the District of Columbia itself. Pastoral Widow's Mite had been a part of Maryland as early as the 1600s and, according to the Kalorama Citizens Association bulletin of September 1966: "Before 1764 a colonist had built a plantation house on Kalorama hill overlooking Rock Creek. That stream was then wide and deep and unbridged. Seagoing ships sailed it far beyond the present zoo. The plantation owner cut a wide oblique access down the hill to a floating dock, and all travel to and from the house was by boat."

When the federal government moved to Washington in 1800,

Joel Barlow, a poet, pamphleteer, and diplomat who negotiated the treaty ending America's war with the Barbary pirates, bought the plantation and named it Kalorama—loosely taken from the Greek word for "beautiful view." Poor Barlow was subsequently sent by President James Madison to work out a commercial treaty with Napoleon. By one account Barlow passed Napoleon on the road in the midst of his retreat from Russia and died of pneumonia in a peasant's cottage near Cracow; in another version, he froze to death in a blizzard.

Kalorama became a magnet for many of the nation's "political, military, and social elite, as well as foreign chanceries and official residences," wrote historian Patrick Andrus in a National Park Service report on the neighborhood's national significance. "The district has served as the home to five former presidents (Taft, Wilson, Harding, Hoover, and Roosevelt), Cabinet members, Congressmen, Senators, Supreme Court Justices (Charles Evans Hughes, Louis Brandeis, Harlan Stone, and Joseph Mc-Kenna), high-ranking military officers, and the city's legal, financial and social elite." The quality of individual buildings, "the attention given to siting and landscape design, and the intentional merging and contrasting of styles resulted in a sophisticated ensemble reflective of both the social status of its residents and the growing emergence of Washington, D.C., as one of the world's great cities."

When the Portuguese acquired the second Lawrence house, they greatly enlarged and remodeled it under the direction of architect Frederick Brooke. The interior was decorated by Portuguese architect Leonardo Castro Freire, according to the embassy's own description, "in order to obtain a truly Portuguese atmosphere. The style is inspired by the later part of the 18th century which corresponds to an epoch of great artistic developments in Portugal."

The ambassador's home has been a much enjoyed feast for the visitor's eye. Its entrance hall of Portuguese marble from Estremoz, walls tiled to match the old collegiate church at Coimbra University, chandeliers and wall lamps of the 18th-century King Joao V period, and 17th- and 18th-century maps of the nation, not to mention paintings and objects reflecting Portugal's proud seafaring tradition, are conversation pieces of the first order. With the arrival in the early 1990s of Ambassador José M. Pereira Bastos, who had held diplomatic posts in Denmark, India, Nepal, Bangladesh, Afghanistan, Sri Lanka, and France, the artifacts in the house—representative souvenirs from each of the ambassador's stops—reflect an even greater international diversity.

When Portugal acquired the Kalorama Road house in 1945, architect Leonardo Freire added a "Portuguese atmosphere" in a massive redecoration, later abetted by artwork and statuary.

"'THE GLORY THAT WAS GREECE, AND THE GRAN-
deur that was Rome' were nothing," reported the *Washington Post* in
1933, "compared to the magnificence that was Russia when a Russian
Ambassador held forth in regal splendor in the days of the Tsar." The
ambassador's post, three blocks from the White House, was a five-
story, stone and beige-brick house built by New York architect Nathan
Wyeth for Hattie Sanger Pullman, widow of the Chicago sleeping-car
magnate. (Wyeth's other Washington credits are the Key Bridge,
Columbia Hospital for Women, and the White House's Oval Office.)
Many years later, the Beaux Arts structure would get a tepid review
from the U.S. Commission of Fine Arts: "The Pullman residence as designed by Wyeth is an attempt at originality, if only because it is not
historically 'correct.' Neither is it exceptional for its time, unless size
and costliness of materials are criteria for excellence."

Hattie Pullman, an energetic businesswoman and philanthropist, "is said to have blown three million dollars in an abortive attempt
to crash society here in the Wilson era," according to Robert Smith and
Eric Sevareid in *Washington: Magnificent Capital*. She intended the house
for her daughter and son-in-law, Congressman Frank O. Lowden, but
neither Mrs. Pullman nor the Lowdens ever lived at 1125 16th Street.
Neither did its next owner, Natalie Harris Hammond, who, with her
husband, John Hays Hammond, had a perfectly comfortable mansion
(now the French ambassador's residence) on Kalorama Road. Within
six months in 1913, she sold the 16th Street building for $350,000 to the
government of imperial Russia, which immediately also bought the lot
next door on which to build a chancery.

Over from the old czarist embassy on Rhode Island Avenue
strode Ambassador George Bakhmeteff, who had married an American, Marie Beale, a Washington millionaire and daughter of the owner
of Decatur House (see page 13). Marie Bakhmeteff put her staff of 40
(not counting the chef and kitchen help) to work taking care of the 64-
room house. Came the Russian Revolution in 1917, the Bakhmeteffs re-
paired to their house in Paris, followed by a shipment of the Pullman
house's best antiques, spared from the Bolshevik onslaught. For a time
the provisional government led by Alexander Kerensky, which itself
was busy dodging the Bolsheviks, maintained the house with Bakhmeteff still theoretically on the job. Having little else to do, the caretaker
staff was spotted amazing Washingtonians with their skating prowess
on nearby ponds and neighborhood rinks.

The U.S. government broke diplomatic relations with the Soviets in 1922, the caretakers disappeared, and the embassy sat empty, its
furnishings gathering dust, for 12 years. Once during that time, someone strung a huge banner across the entranceway reading, "Rasputin
closed this embassy. But he opens at Loew's Columbia—'Rasputin and
the Empress.'" In 1933 a moving van pulled up, and workers removed
boxes of papers from the days of the imperial regime. After the Roosevelt administration recognized the Stalinist government a year later, the
building was reopened by new Communist occupants.

Stalin's ambassador, Alexander Troyanovsky, unshuttered the

CHANCERY AND RESIDENCE
OF THE AMBASSADOR
OF THE RUSSIAN REPUBLIC
Pullman House
1125 16th Street, Northwest
Nathan Wyeth, Architect
1910

*The Soviets turned
Hattie Pullman's
Edwardian ballroom,
with its elaborate
columns and cande-
labra—now electri-
fied—into a reception
room, but the tradition
of utterly bourgeois
festivities lived on.*

Pullman house for a gala opening party, where the flag of the hammer and sickle was unfurled and Mrs. Woodrow Wilson, Secretary of State and Mrs. Cordell Hull, and lawyer Clarence Darrow were among the glitterati. Secretary of Labor Frances Perkins, another guest, celebrated her birthday in the midst of four floors of buffet lines. So envious were the uninvited that several donned formal attire and tried to crash the party, but, according to Hope Ridings Miller, "a platoon of door checkers barred the uninvited proletariat, and the rebuffed contingent had to take an embarrassed exit through a throng of curious spectators jamming 16th Street."

The guests could not help but notice a huge portrait of Comrade Stalin hanging incongruously in the vortex of capitalist excess, the Versailles-inspired ballroom. By 1959, when Premier Nikita Khrushchev paid a visit and threw a party of his own for the Eisenhowers and a few hundred friends, Stalin's portrait was nowhere to be found. For the Khrushchev affair, the Soviets borrowed the Mayflower Hotel's fabled gold service, flew in the chef and most of the food from Moscow, and topped off the evening with servings of Baked Alaska (an attempt at a lighthearted bow to the former Russian outpost), each topped with a red (what else?) twinkling, battery-powered light.

The Pullman house had been refurbished by New York architect Eugene Schoen when the Communists first moved in. He was instructed to decorate it in an Art Moderne style but declined, saying it would be sinful to tear out gilded and rococo furnishings that would cost $2.5 million (in 1933 dollars) to replace. Vowing he would not touch "the last hair of the last cupid," Schoen stuck to pedestrian improvements like a central vacuum-cleaning system and new kitchens and baths.

By Cold War days of the 1950s through the 1970s, two other characteristics of the building stood out: its array of 12 antennae on the mansard roof (the Soviets were doing more than watching Walter Cronkite), and the closed and heavily draped windows. As the thermostat seemed to be perpetually set at 80 degrees, whatever the weather, one visitor called the embassy "the most overheated building since those destroyed in the Chicago fire." At an embassy party marking the publication of a cookbook on Russian cuisine, writer Cleveland Amory, remarking on the abundance of non-Slavic chowhounds and paucity of Soviet hosts, cracked, "They're all upstairs taking showers because the air is so bad in here."

There were a few, but only a few, other parties for outsiders hosted by the suspicious Soviets in their gold-braided uniforms. One, in honor

---

When the Soviets and Americans finally established diplomatic relations after a 12-year hiatus, Stalin quickly sent over his new ambassador to the United States. The *Washington Daily News*'s Evelyn Peyton Gordon described Washington's reaction: "When Ambassador Alexander Antonovich Troyanovsky set foot here, Washingtonians were surprised that he didn't wear a long beard and carry a knife in his teeth," she wrote. "Such were our ideas of the new regime of Russia." Americans had formed some of their notions of Russianness from the imperial minister to Washington in President John Tyler's day, 90 years earlier. Baron de Bodisco was a bachelor in his late 50s and a regular at Henry Clay's poker games. One night he arose from the game, down $1,000. "Ladees and gentlemans," the *Washington Times-Herald* quotes him as having said, "it is very disagree duty to make it announce that these receptions must have an end and to declare them at an end for the present because why? The fund for them ladees and gentlemans is exhaust." The baron recovered sufficient funds to wed the 16-year-old daughter of the U.S. adjutant general. The *Times-Herald* story described the radiant bride, the groom in "dyed whiskers and hair," the groomsmen, all over 50 and some "tottering on the verge of septuagenarianism," and the bridesmaids, all aged 14 to 16.

---

of the Apollo-Soyuz space flight in 1975 and attended by the cosmonauts and astronauts, featured a four-foot-high cheese rocket. The most extravagant bash of all occurred each October, ironically celebrating the revolution of the proletariat. One party was described by *Collier's* writer Andrew Tully as laying out "enough fancy food and liquor to nourish and intoxicate a Russian village for a month."

When Soviet Ambassador Georgi Nikolayevich Zaroubin presented his credentials to President Harry Truman in 1952, he announced that he would like to promote peace and take in a Washington Senators' baseball game. "Georgi Zaroubin can be as charming as he likes, but he's not kidding anybody," Tully wrote. "The people who deal with him know his background, and after he shakes their hand they always check to see how many fingers they've got left." That background included tours of duty in Canada when a spy ring was exposed and in Great Britain when Klaus Fuchs confessed to passing atomic-energy secrets to the Kremlin.

The 500-member Soviet diplomatic staff, the largest in Washington, lived painfully circumscribed lives. The staff was forbidden to mix with the population; all but the ambassador required approval to see a movie or accept a dinner invitation. Except on Revolution Day, the only sanctioned embassy parties involved diplomats from the Eastern Bloc nations, where, Tully reported, the Russians looked down on their colleagues, "and the satellites in turn defer to the Russians and, often, hate their guts." Entertainment—typically somber music and turgid films—was a study in drabness. Only the top embassy staff was permitted time off for a visit to Rehoboth Beach, Delaware, site of a summer diplomatic colony, where, presumably, KGB minions in bathing suits kept a close eye on them. Several Soviet diplomatic families lived in connecting communal houses on 21st Street; their youngsters, eight and under, studied Russian and French but were forbidden to learn English; older children were shipped back to the Soviet Union for a proper education. Whenever touch-up work was needed inside the old Pullman house, guards watched the workers' every move. One sentry was reported to have told a painter, "Please, comrade, don't blame us. We don't even trust ourselves."

Security precautions were prudent, as protesters regularly demonstrated outside. In 1968 a bomb, tossed before dawn, took a chunk out of the building's stone sills and iron grillwork.

Beginning in 1962, both the Soviet and U.S. governments laid plans for new facilities in each other's capitals. After two unsuccessful at-

A portrait of V. I. Lenin outlasted, at least for a time, the "Second Russian Revolution" that ousted the Communist leadership in 1991 as envoys struggled with an uncertain national identity.

tempts to locate a new embassy compound in residential areas of the District of Columbia, the Soviets did succeed in finding space, including the Nathaniel Luttrell mansion at Connecticut Avenue and Columbia Road. Finally an almost brick-for-brick reciprocal deal was cut in 1969 to build a new U.S. embassy in Moscow (what became the famous "bug"-infested structure built but never occupied) and a sprawling Soviet government complex on Mount Alto, the highest point in the city. The land, offered rent-free for 85 years, is on the 12.5-acre site of a former veterans' hospital not far from the Washington National Cathedral. Workers were

closely supervised; technicians from Moscow installed every electronic component (including an even more impressive array of antennae). The embassy ordered the windows fabricated on site rather than at a factory. American and Soviet workers on the project shared their lunch hours in nearby Wisconsin Avenue taverns, where vodka outsold beer three to one.

At first it seemed that the Soviets would unload the Pullman house as a decadent reminder of their nation's czarist past. Senator Joseph Montoya of New Mexico, whose profession was real estate, tried to buy the building, but Ambassador Anatoly Dobrynin declined, saying his government would keep the 16th Street address "as a recreation center for our staff." Indeed the Soviets kept it, for the State Department forbade their moving the chancery or the ambassador's residence to Mount Alto until its own second try at building an eavesdropping-proof embassy in Moscow was complete.

The dorms and peripheral facilities at the new embassy were in use, however, during Mikhail Gorbachev's historic period of *glasnost* and *perestroika,* as well as the astounding "Second Russian Revolution"—the failed Moscow coup of 1991 that accelerated the dissolution of the Communist empire. It was during this period that we took our photographs for *Embassies of Washington.* A huge portrait of Vladimir Lenin, hanging at the top of the sweeping grand staircase, was still much in evidence, and an embassy official explained that, whether or not Communism was in its death throes, hundreds of thousands of Soviet citizens had given their lives in Lenin's name at the walls of Leningrad. Since then, the Soviet embassy has become the Embassy of the Russian Republic, with office space offered to other republics until further arrangements can be made. Left unclear was the prognosis for a curtain over the proscenium arch at the new embassy's 400-seat theater, on which had been stitched a slogan: "Forward the Victory of Communism."

Two other vestiges of a discredited era marked the old Pullman House: the Soviet hammer-and-sickle flag and an array of antennae once employed for far more than improving television reception.

THE EMBASSIES OF WASHINGTON ARE KNOWN FOR their monumental architecture, their colorful human legacies, their lavish social encounters, and their intrigue. But one diplomatic building, housing the ambassador of the Republic of South Africa, is renowned for a single room. The building, erected in 1936 to house the South African legation before it achieved embassy status, features a dining room paneled in rare native "stinkhout," or stinkwood. The now-rare, rock-hard, walnut-like wood, which shows up in expensive desks and bookcases throughout the house, takes two centuries to mature, so it is vigorously protected. The name of the *Ocotea bullata* tree comes from the rancid odor of the wood when it is first cut.

The residence was designed by architect John J. Whelan, who, five years earlier, had supervised erection of the Norwegian legation farther up Massachusetts Avenue. According to an embassy publication, Minister Ralph Close admonished Whelan to be sure "the exterior should, without being in any way ornate, at least be chaste and dignified and such as South Africans can reasonably be proud of." The intent was to feature the 18th-century Cape Dutch architecture of the Cape of Good Hope, but Indiana limestone was substituted for the traditional whitewashed plaster. The building's portico is a replica of the Kat balcony in the pentagonal castle in Cape Town, built by the Dutch East India Company in the 17th century.

Architect Whelan designed not only the building but also the residence's dining-room tables and chairs. Old Cape Dutch cabinets, breakfronts, trousseau "kists," or chests, and paintings by South African artists have been added by ambassadors over the years. Among these are depictions of a Transvaal landscape, a Cape Town fishing scene, and a series of Zulu portraits. A chancery annex, completed in 1965, is reached through the second-floor library. It is a replica of an 18th-century Dutch homestead.

Not surprisingly, considering the international tumult sparked by South Africa's apartheid policies, the embassy compound has been a frequent target of protests. Free South Africa movement leaders and celebrities, including, in 1975, singer Stevie Wonder, have periodically been arrested for demonstrating within 500 feet of an embassy. "What happens when an embassy becomes beleaguered?" asked the *Washington Star*'s Joy Billington in 1978. "Do important people still go to that ambassador's parties, or do they tend to avoid them? The answer appears to be that most Washingtonians don't care about politics, providing the 'lamb chop' is well cooked and the wines good."

The "lamb chop" reference was to the "Lamb Chop Principle," articulated, according to Billington, by either the late famous Washington hostess Perle Mesta or the noted journalist Joseph Alsop, that a good meal and pleasant company will always draw a crowd. Without doubt, South African ambassadors have had a more taxing challenge than most to explain their country's policies. As apartheid laws are dismantled by the Pretoria government, the task of representing the nation in Washington figures to get smoother.

RESIDENCE OF
THE AMBASSADOR OF
SOUTH AFRICA
3101 Massachusetts Avenue, Northwest
John J. Whelan, Architect
1936

*Following pages:
Stinkwood, from which
the South African
ambassador's dining-
room paneling, chairs,
table, and buffet
are carved, is now a
carefully protected flora.
Ceramic and clay
figures, clay pots, and
ostrich-egg beads dot
the residence.*

RESIDENCE OF THE AMBASSADOR OF SPAIN

A Henderson House
2801 16th Street, Northwest
George Oakley Totten, Architect

═══ 1923 ═══

The Spanish ambassador's patio is an imitation of a typical Andalusian courtyard, with its window ironwork, tiled floor, fountain, and tiled portrait of the Blessed Virgin.

THE STORY OF THIS ELEGANT AMBASSADORIAL residence is enmeshed in a tale of *Gone with the Wind* proportions, complete with its own Tara and headstrong female lead.

Inside Boundary Castle, the turreted brownstone fortress that dominated the west side of the 2200 block of 16th Street at the turn of the century, the woman whom the *Washington Star* called "Washington's social arbiter," Mary Foote Henderson, hatched a grand plan: to build, on hundreds of surrounding acres, several other manor houses and rent them, or sell them at cost, to foreign governments as showplaces for their diplomatic corps, thus creating a glorious Embassy Hill on Meridian Heights (later, Hill) and cleaning up the seedy neighborhood. As early as 1890, Mary Henderson and her husband, John—the former U.S. senator from Missouri, friend of Abraham Lincoln, and author of the Thirteenth Amendment abolishing slavery—methodically began to purchase more than 300 parcels of land surrounding the castle, sweeping away shanties, meager vegetable plots, and unsightly billboards as they went. From his days in banking and real estate, the senator had amassed a fortune reputed to exceed $20 million. When he was voted out of office for siding with Andrew Johnson in the president's impeachment proceedings, Henderson told his wife, according to a story in *The American Weekly,* "We have nothing to worry about. My fortune is your fortune. We'll enjoy it."

The view from the castle on Boundary Street (now Florida Avenue) on the upper ridge of Washington civility, down to the White House and Washington Monument, had been anything but the most majestic in the low-lying capital, but after her husband's death in 1913, Mary Foote Henderson determined to make it so. Having once founded an art school in St. Louis, she retained an amateur's interest in architecture. After drawing her own preliminary sketches of the diplomats' homes, she dipped into the Henderson fortune and commissioned her favorite architect, George Oakley Totten, Jr., and others to build a dozen separate villas on the heights. "When a diplomat desires a new home in Washington, his thoughts turn towards Mrs. Henderson," wrote G. L. Waddell in the *National Republic* in 1927. "He holds a consultation with the brisk little mistress of Boundary Castle, and before long, there is another national crest displayed on Embassy Hill."

All the while, the widow Henderson carried the torch for her rehabilitated main street. Wrote James M. Goode in *Capital Losses,* "It was a familiar sight to see her with her gardener planting shrubbery along 16th Street." She convinced city commissioners to rename 16th Street "Avenue of the Presidents" but could savor the victory all too briefly. Annoyed at having to alter their stationery and house signs and to hunt for 16th Street between 15th and 17th, her neighbors quickly got "Avenue of the Presidents" changed back to its more prosaic designation.

Beginning with a new embassy for France, however, Mary Henderson's diplomatic colony sprouted nicely and soon included stately homes for the ministers of Ecuador, Spain, Mexico, Cuba, Poland, Lithuania, and the Netherlands. Most had been designed from the start

with the architecture of the host nation in mind. One that was not was the Spanish embassy, which, because of another Henderson brainstorm, was of "American" design. In 1922 Henderson formally offered to donate the palatial residence that Totten was building on the east side of the 2800 block of 16th Street to the federal government as a vice presidential château. No way, huffed Florence Harding, the nation's First Lady. There would not be any regal billeting for a mere vice president: "Do you think I'm going to have those Coolidges living in a home like *that*?" she exclaimed. Congress, too, did not believe that the vice president, then quietly ensconced at the Willard Hotel, could afford the lifestyle that went with such quarters, donated or otherwise, and declined the offer.

The pipe dream of a vice presidential château, on top of Mary Henderson's earlier fancy, also rejected, that the presidential family itself ought to move to Meridian Hill, sounded an alarm with her granddaughter and only heir, Beatrice Henderson Wholean. It was not difficult to come up with proven eccentricities with which to tar the old dowager, for the headstrong Mary Henderson had drained the contents of Henderson Castle's renowned wine cellar into the 16th Street gutter in a show of support for Prohibition; railed against flesh-toned silk stockings and high-heeled shoes and required her maids to wear almost floor-length Victorian skirts well into the age of "flappers"; so disdained meat that she once served bananas shaped to look like pork chops; attacked the "poison vices" of "the drunkard, the glutton and the tobacco hog" in the best-known of her many books, the 700-page *The Aristocracy of Health;* ridden, twice a day, to the Lincoln Memorial, where she would walk twice around its reflecting pool; and, also twice, been hauled before a District of Columbia judge for cutting down trees that obstructed her view of the White House.

The Red Living Room was the ballroom in what was originally envisioned as a U.S. vice president's abode. The 18th-century painting over the fireplace is of Queen Isabel Farnesio, wife of Philip V.

What, asked Beatrice Wholean, was to prevent this dervish, when she'd finished giving away buildings to official Washington, from frivolously dissipating all of her holdings? The granddaughter sought to have her institutionalized, only to lose her courtroom standing when Mary Henderson proved her to be an adoptee without the proper bloodlines for such a challenge. (After Henderson's death, at 90, at her summer home in Maine in 1931, the $6 million estate was left to her Japanese private secretary, Jesse S. Shima, who, after yet another court challenge that delighted society-page voyeurs, eventually divvied it up with granddaughter Beatrice.)

Mary Foote Henderson's vice presidential pretensions for 2801 16th Street having faded, she began touting the property as an ideal embassy for the government of Mexico, then seeking a location, but Mexico selected another estate altogether just up the street in the same block as 2801, and Totten's cavernous creation stood empty for three years. In 1926 the Spanish government—already a Henderson tenant at 2620 16th—decided to move its embassy to 2801. The Spaniards soon added to the main building a winter garden, fountain, hand-painted tiles from Seville and Valencia, wrought-iron doors and grilles from Toledo, and wainscoting. Construction also began on a new chancery (designed by a different architect, Jules Henri de Sibour), with an entrance facing in the other direction, on 15th Street. Particularly striking on the main building's patio-conservatory to this day is a mosaic of the Madonna de Los Reyes, patroness of Seville.

Although Hope Ridings Miller described the white stone Spanish embassy as having been inspired by "a Venetian palace," it is snootily dismissed, in *Homes of Interest In and Around Washington,* as "grand adobe style," with "badly scaled Beaux-Arts attachments" that work into a "California mission" look. The "frenzy of balustrades which in Totten's enthusiasm wrap about the facade and down the elliptical drive . . . do serve a happy purpose," the author states, in that they "draw attention away from details that, with height, decrease in quality."

The Spanish embassy has been redecorated several times since 1949. It had fallen into disrepair from 1936 to 1939, during the nation's civil war, a *Washington Daily News* reporter noting that the ballroom had been turned into a storeroom but was finally "taking shape as a beautiful drawing room." Paintings by Spanish masters, including Goya, and 17th-century Flemish tapestries continue to enhance the interior.

Further renovation in 1955 was supervised by Archduke Franz Josef of Spain and his wife, Princess Marta, who had established an interior-decorating shop in New York. "French is the diplomatic language, so I will make the ballroom a French room, all crystally and white and gold," the princess told the *Evening Star.* Ambassador José Maria Areilza also rehung the large portraits of King Alfonso XIII and Queen Victoria Eugenia that had been removed in 1931 with the end of the Spanish monarchy.

Other ambassadors and their wives have since made alterations to the patio-conservatory and have added flocked silk wall coverings in the drawing room and ballroom, where chandeliers from La Granja crystal works near Segovia, Spain, and Flemish tapestries also hang. Prominent during the tenure of several envoys have been artworks on loan from the Prado or brought from previous tours of duty in South America. "Badly scaled" or not, the Spanish embassy has been a featured station on the Washington diplomatic trail, and the Spaniards have liked it so well that they have stayed in one spot longer than any other foreign government.

As for Mary Foote Henderson's sandstone castle that started it all, it outlasted the feisty dowager by 18 years. When it was razed in 1949, only the entrance posts were left standing.

A silver urn is one of many Spanish touches added by ambassadors and their wives to what George Oakley Totten had originally designed as one of his few strictly "American" houses.

RESIDENCE OF THE
AMBASSADOR OF SWEDEN

David Lawrence House

3900 Nebraska Avenue, Northwest

Arthur Heaton, Architect

1923

Architect Arthur Heaton was inspired by Spanish architecture when he designed this house on Nebraska Avenue. The three crowns—Sweden's national symbol—are one of the few exterior Swedish embellishments.

SIR WILLIAM GILBERT, OF GILBERT AND SULLIVAN, had a point when he wrote, "Things are seldom what they seem," and you can prove it at the Swedish ambassador's residence in Washington. The home, designed for *U.S. News & World Report* founder David Lawrence by architect Arthur Heaton in 1923, is a full-blown Spanish-style hacienda, complete with red-tiled roof, set on eight acres of impeccably landscaped grounds—hardly the place you'd expect to hail Sweden's Martin's Goose Day or sip mulled glögg on the feast of Saint Lucia. There are even Mexican tin plates and a large Spanish refectory table inside to complete the effect, and the cultural confusion continues with Flemish tapestries—bought at auction by a previous ambassador—and a brass Buddha. To be sure, the residence abounds in Swedish glassware, chandeliers, and royal portraits as well. Above the entrance door is the Swedish coat of arms with its distinctive three crowns—representing the Scandinavian kingdoms of Sweden, Denmark, and Norway, which were united for more than 120 years, beginning with a treaty signed in the Swedish city of Kalmar in 1397. Superseding the trio of crowns is the larger royal diadem of King Erik of Pomerania, overall ruler of the Nordic union.

The Swedes, who bought the house from Lawrence in 1950, know that unexpected contrasts are endemic to a nation that stretches from Baltic ports to Lapland, where the first snow may fall in August and the last in early June. The change of seasons alone is a matter for wonderment, and at no other embassy is the coming of spring—marked by the April 30 Feast of Valborg—so ebulliently toasted, with a paean to the distant and budding Virginia hills on the other side of the Potomac River.

The Swedes serve up some of diplomatic Washington's most anticipated cuisine, prepared by the chef in his own small house off the walled garden. A smorgasbord might offer a choice among such national dishes as jellied pig's feet, reindeer meat, goose-blood soup, or sour herring, which, a Swedish Institute handbook, *Traditional Festivities in Sweden,* points out, results from "controlled rotting" of the fish after their hermetically sealed tins have turned "distinctly 'swollen'" by the time they are ready for sale." Sardonically, the author adds, "A pungent aroma—delectable to some, repulsive to others—fills the room whenever a can is opened." When the Christmas gnome is about, a stack of deep-fried Swedish rosettes, drenched in powdered sugar, makes up for any indignity.

If the mind plays tricks at the Royal Swedish embassy, so do the Swedes, for whom practical jokes are a delicious diversion. Only in Sweden would an entire television network attempt to fool the nation into believing it could turn its black-and-white television sets into color models by stretching nylon hosiery over the screens. To the owners of thousands of ruined stockings on that Första April, the network announced, "April Fool!" It's a bit like the sensation one gets opening the door of the hacienda on Nebraska Avenue any night of the year and finding the pragmatic people who represent what Marquis Childs once called "Sweden, the middle way."

RESIDENCE OF THE
AMBASSADOR OF TURKEY

The Everett House
1606 23rd Street, Northwest
George Oakley Totten, Jr., Architect

1915

IF EVER THERE WAS MUSIC TO AN ARCHITECT'S
ears, it was the words uttered in 1914 by multimillionaire Edward Ham-
lin Everett when he commissioned George Oakley Totten to build a
home on Sheridan Circle: "Cost is no object! And style and design are
up to you."

Everett earned his walking-around money in Texas oil and Missouri beer, but he made his fortune on his patent for the simple crimped
cap that sealed millions of bottles of that beer, and soft drinks, from
coast to coast at a time when almost every American city had at least
one brewery. The "Bottle-Top King" had met Totten through Everett's
friends the Hendersons at the time the architect was helping Mary
Foote Henderson turn upper 16th Street into Embassy Row.

Ironically, Totten had spent time in Constantinople, where he
was about to embark on another dream commission as Sultan Abdul-
Hamid II's personal architect—just as the Young Turk rebellion
brought down the Ottoman ruler—so Totten returned to Washington
and built mansions for Mary Henderson instead.

On the site of a former city dump, the brick and Bowling Green
granite home he designed had architectural details from three centuries.
The "cost is no object" imprint was clearly evident in the ornate ball-

National hero Mustafa
Kemal Atatürk's bust
looms on a landing.
Opposite:
"Bottle-Top King"
Edward Everett told
his architect
to damn the cost for
his new mansion.
Following page:
Vases add color
to the building's stone-
walled sunroom.

97

room with coffered ceiling, and the house's stained-glass bays, hand-carved staircase, billiard room, velvet-covered walls, teakwood floors, basement swimming pool, and roof garden with a spectacular view of the city. Many exterior details, from the fluted columns to ornate portico, suggest homes Totten saw during his stay on the Bosporus.

The "Bottle-Top King" met operatic soprano Grace Burnap at a Henderson party in 1919 and married her. According to Henry Mitchell's *Houses of the Capital,* the Everetts entertained lavishly and were famous for their gala "Evenings with Music" at which Grace and other opera stars performed.

Everett lived in his new mansion until his death in 1929; Grace stayed on three years more. In 1932 the Republic of Turkey leased the house with the prospect of buying it, although Henderson was dangling one of her uptown castles before the Turks as well. A year or so later they opted to stay where they were, buying the Everett mansion and all its furnishings, adding over the years their own Turkish rugs, crystal, and a gigantic bronze head of the republic's founder, Mustafa Kemal Atatürk.

The irony was complete: Turks would live in a spectacular George Oakley Totten house after all.

In 1955, long after the house had become the Turkish embassy, Ambassador Haydar Gork almost literally stumbled on the swimming pool, which had been boarded over by an earlier delegation. He unsealed it, had fluorescent lights installed overhead, and painted the walls and ceilings. "Not that the Turkish Embassy needs the luxury of a swimming pool," Ambassador Gork told Evelyn Peyton Gordon of the *Washington Daily News.* "But since it is there, why not use it!"

THE HEDGES AND WARRENS OF THE HEATH AROUND
Observatory Circle, "way out" Massachusetts Avenue, were just the
ticket for the British early in the 1920s, when they scouted a spot for a
massive new embassy compound. They'd been the first foreign nation
to build a Washington embassy, on Connecticut Avenue at N Street in
1872, when that, too, was countryside, full of leftover Civil War bar-
racks, brick kilns, and free-running pigs.

The cornerstone for the new $700,000 compound was laid on
June 3, 1928, the 63rd birthday of King George V; his royal crest, a crown
atop the monogram GVR (George V Rex), is chiseled into the building's
limestone trim. The U.S. Commission of Fine Arts, which scoured city
records to discover the previous owner of the property, had little luck,
concluding only that it had been held by a trust from the area's days as
part of far-flung Pretty Prospect. A 1927 *Washington Times* article
identified the landowner as Harry Wardman, a native of England, whom
it called "a Washington capitalist" and who, it said, not only reaped a
profit from the sale but also gained title to the former embassy property
as well as submitting the low bid to construct the new building.

The new limestone and red-brick manor house, with its towering
chimneys, that rose on four and a half acres under the direction of Sir Edwin Lutyens, is usually described as a Queen Anne–style country house.
(E. J. Applewhite in *Washington Itself* calls it "almost pompous.") The
chancery annex, added in 1960, brought the number of rooms in the
complex to 400, so that, from the air, it looks like a small university. Indeed, the columned grand porch attached to the four-story ambassador's
residence out back would be the envy of many a campus. For Sir Edward, who had designed the imperial viceroy's palace in New Delhi, the
South African war memorial in Johannesburg, and London's Whitehall
memorial to the unknown soldier of World War I, the Washington embassy was his only work in the Western Hemisphere. For the British embassy, Lutyens copied design elements he had used in the New Delhi
palace, and he ordered the house's bricks handmade in Pennsylvania to
approximate those of Tudor England. "The spirit of old England breathes
from the structure," wrote the *Washington Post* soon after it opened.

"Though other embassies in Washington are counted more romantic or spectacular or beautiful," opined the *Post* later in 1976, "for
solid impressiveness, the British Embassy overpowers them all. . . . The
British Embassy reflects all the glory of the British Empire during those
years and the grandeur of its never setting sun. Today, when Great
Britain has lost its far flung crown jewels of countries, the need for the
grandiose space still exists, not only for its obvious 'chins up' boost to
the spirits, but also because Britain still maintains the largest staff of
any country in Washington, though the Soviet Union counts more
officers with diplomatic rank."

The U-shaped chancery fronts on the avenue, behind four gateways framed by gateposts. "Those In and Out to the Chancery [are]
capped by urns," notes Applewhite, "those In and Out to the residence
capped by lions and unicorns. This is a design for Rolls Royces, not
pedestrians." The residence is joined to the chancery by a porte coch-

CHANCERY AND RESIDENCE
OF THE AMBASSADOR OF
THE UNITED KINGDOM OF
GREAT BRITAIN AND
NORTHERN IRELAND
3100 Massachusetts Avenue, Northwest
Sir Edwin Lutyens, Architect
1930

ère, surmounted by the embassy library and social secretary's office.

The ambassador's several gardens have been the subject of many articles, including one in 1976 by the *Washington Post*'s Henry Mitchell, in which he lauds the gardens' civility: "Nowhere was there that ruinous babble of walkie-talkies and if the British have a public-address system, they had the grace never to use it. Nothing ruins a garden sooner than a batch of microphones, unless it is a batch of loons lecturing over them. None of these abtruded, nothing to break the spell or the wild fantasy that people can be civilized and happy and at peace without any effort at all in a rush of roses."

In front of the garden, with one foot on British soil and the other planted in the District of Columbia (symbolizing his Anglo-American parentage and honorary U.S. citizenship), stands the bronze statue of Sir Winston Churchill, by the American sculptor William McVey. The late prime minister is shown flashing his famous V-for-Victory sign with one hand and clutching a good-sized cigar in the other.

The embassy had hardly been christened when a Conservative, Commander A. R. J. Southby, rose in the dock to protest the $150,000 worth of extra land it had been necessary to purchase for the ever-growing building. Is it true, he asked, "that the design is as bad as popular report says, that the heating pipes go through the larders, that the garage accommodation is hopelessly insufficient for the use of the ambassador and his staff, and that, therefore, fresh expenditure is to be incurred by the taxpayer, to provide accommodations which should have been thought of at the time?"

The new British embassy began a trend. While one or two embassies had already located on close-in Massachusetts Avenue, there was a veritable stampede to locate on the extended avenue once the British moved in. Brazil, Norway, South Africa, the Vatican, and Venezuela followed Britain there in the 1930s, and several others moved just around one or another corner nearby. Effectively, they moved Embassy Row from 16th Street.

The hottest invitation in town, save for one from the White House, quickly became a summons to the British embassy for strawberries, Devonshire cream, and champagne to toast the monarch's birthday. In 1949, the ambassador, Sir Oliver Franks, mindful of a recent devaluing of the pound back home, cut a few corners by substituting tea and cookies for the strawberries, cream, and bubbly. He never heard the end of it, and it was budget-be-damned the next year and ever since. Although the British are unequaled at pomp and polish, someone overdid the preparations for the visit of Prime Minister Harold Wilson in 1970. So diligently buffed was the floor of the embassy's marble corridor that Wilson skidded into an indecorous pratfall. A guard was soon posted outside reception rooms to warn guests to be careful.

King George VI was the first British monarch to make a state visit to the United States and to visit the new embassy. Because all of their visits have been state visits, Queen Elizabeth II and Prince Philip, while entertaining often at the embassy, have always stayed at Blair House, the official residence near the White House for foreign digni-

Prime Minister Harold Wilson once took a tumble on the squares of shiny slate and Vermont marble of the main corridor that passes the British embassy's library and ballroom.
Opposite:
The embassy's fabled gardens deliver an equine surprise.

The embassy's library is almost a cube. Its woodwork is liquidambar, a variety of California gum. Architect Lutyens disliked ornamentation, and designer David Hicks's furnishings are faithful to that spirit.

taries visiting the U.S. president. Other British notables, however, including the Prince and Princess of Wales, have been overnight guests at the embassy.

Among the many Americans who have attended events at the British embassy were the two children of President and Mrs. John F. Kennedy, Caroline and "John-John," who attended a small, private nursery school there during the early 1960s when Sir David Ormsby Gore was ambassador.

For conviviality, no one has topped the first couple to occupy the U.K. residence. Sir Ronald Charles and Lady Elizabeth Lindsay—the latter Long Island–born and a trained landscape artist whose talents were put to good use in the embassy's gardens—gave an average of four dinners a month, plus uncounted receptions and balls. Sir Ronald, Hope Miller wrote in *Embassy Row,* was a "paragon of the traditional British diplomat in the Kitchener era, sent out to carry on among a bunch of colonials [and] a hulk of a man with a walrus mustache and an aloof air. He had no conception that the sun was setting on the British Empire; but in his ceremonial uniform, heavily weighted with decorations including the Order of the Garter, he was monumental."

As for the witty Lady Elizabeth, Miller noted that she suggested her own epitaph: "Served by all; of service to none; died of the tea hour."

IT WAS NATURAL, IN 1939, FOR REPRESENTATIVES of the Vatican to turn to architect Frank Vernon Murphy to create a dignified new diplomatic mission on Massachusetts Avenue's Observatory Circle. Murphy, chairman of the architecture department at Catholic University in Washington, had designed several structures on that campus, as well as church buildings for several denominations from Baltimore to Toledo.

The new nunciature—then called the Apostolic Delegation—was built 10 years after the Italian government recognized the sovereignty of the Holy See and created the independent state of Vatican City. The Vatican had owned the Massachusetts Avenue lot since 1931. Murphy's creation is a three-story Italian Renaissance palazzo of Indiana limestone on a granite base, with a tile roof. It cost $550,000 to build and furnish, and to help pay for it, the *New York Times* noted, "each Catholic diocese in the United States has been assessed according to its resources." The garden courtyard features the bronze Pigna Fountain, in the shape of a fir cone, a one-third-scale reproduction of that in the Cortile della Pigna in the Vatican Museum in Rome.

Murphy, who incorporated stained glass liberally throughout the building, described it as "frankly inspired from the more restrained and dignified of the Italian palaces of the Renaissance." European travelers compared it with the Villa d'Este on Lake Como and the Villa Medici in Rome. One stained-glass window, transported from the mission's cramped Biltmore Street residence, depicts scenes and texts from the "Paradise" section of Dante's *Divine Comedy*. Portraits of popes, cardinals, and saints, including Mother Elizabeth Ann Seton, the first native-born American to be canonized, hang throughout the house. Secular figures, including George Washington and Christopher Columbus, have their places as well.

The nunciature sits across the street from the vice president's residence, catercorner from the British embassy and next door to the Norwegian diplomatic residence. For two decades it was also a neighbor of the "Texas embassy," home of Representative Clark Thompson and his wife, Libby, whose regal entertaining nearly always included priests from the nunciature. In 1991 Finland purchased the Thompson home for $6 million and demolished it to make room for the newest Massachusetts Avenue embassy.

The apostolic delegate who took up residence in Murphy's new edifice, Archbishop Pietro Fumasino Biondi, was described as the "all but official" ambassador, for no diplomatic relations existed between Washington and Vatican City at the time. Officially the mission served instead as a link between American dioceses and the Holy See. Relations had been in hiatus since 1878, when the Italian government absorbed the Papal States into a new, unified Italy. Washington did not resume formal recognition until 1983, after more than 100 other nations had already done so. William A. Wilson was sent as U.S. ambassador to the Holy See; Archbishop Pio Laghi, upon presenting his papers to President Ronald Reagan early the next year, became the pronuncio, while the legation took on the designation "Apostolic Nunciature."

APOSTOLIC NUNCIATURE
OF THE HOLY SEE
(THE VATICAN)
3339 Massachusetts Avenue, Northwest
Frederick Vernon Murphy, Architect
1939

The organization Americans United for Separation of Church and State, two Protestant denominations, and a Catholic lay group filed suit to block diplomatic relations, saying such ties would give preference to "one religious denomination over all others" and thereby violate the First Amendment. Supporters pointed out that an informal diplomatic relationship already existed: George Washington had sent a consul to the Holy See in 1797; James K. Polk had upgraded the office to legation status in 1867; and several U.S. ministers to the Holy See had been confirmed by the Senate. The United States also had diplomatic

The marble fountain in the Nunciature's rear courtyard copies a larger one at the Vatican. Opposite: Stained glass depicts scenes from Dante's DIVINE COMEDY.

relations with the Court of St. James, even though the monarch was head of the Church of England, the Justice Department noted, and the United States and the Holy See had routinely signed international treaties and agreements. Plaintiffs countered by pointing to a speech by Archbishop Laghi, in which he said that the Holy See's authority is spiritual and moral and not dependent upon temporal power. The U.S. government responded that "however the Holy See views itself, it is a highly influential player on the stage of world diplomacy." As a diplomatic player, the nunciature serves as a conduit for information between the Holy See and the U.S. government, as well as the liaison between Roman Catholic churches here and the Vatican.

In accepting an honorary degree from Catholic University in 1984, Archbishop Laghi pointed to the remarks of Pope Paul VI when he served as pro-secretary of state before his elevation: "If diplomacy works through the medium of responsible representatives, if it seeks to construct peace, if it is indeed the art of peace, then no other institution and no other relationship between the peoples more deserves the support of the Catholic Church which, more than any other earthly good, seeks, preaches and gives birth to this peace, true peace."

Archbishop Agostino Cacciavillan, pronuncio to the United States in 1991, reflected on the subject as well: "The art of diplomacy, after all, has everything to do with honest exchange and frank encounter. It does not seek confrontation, but it relies on mutual understanding and is at pains to protect the integrity of that dialog which is the special bond of friendship between those countries which exchange ambassadors. Once you admit that diplomacy exists to promote peace, justice, and mutual cooperation, it seems so natural that the Catholic Church, founded by the Prince of Peace, would have such a venerable and effective posture in world diplomacy."

╪═════╤╔╝╙╤═════╕

RESIDENCE OF THE
AMBASSADOR
OF VENEZUELA

2443 Massachusetts Avenue, Northwest

Chester A. Patterson, Architect

════ *1939* ════

THE VENEZUELAN EMBASSY HAS BEEN THE SCENE of dozens of memorable affairs—masquerade balls, elegant dinners, and receptions—but none more memorable than its first. In 1939 the United States and Venezuela established full diplomatic relations for the first time. In February 1940 Don Diogenes Escalante, the first ambassador of Venezuela, opened the doors of his new official residence for a housewarming. As the *Washington Times-Herald*'s scribe Jean Eliot wrote, the ambassador and his wife "had asked 1,200 guests between the hours of 5 and 8 o'clock. Seemingly none sent regrets, most of them arrived along about 6 o'clock, and the most spectacular traffic jam ever seen at an embassy party was the result." A line of 300 or more people snaked down the driveway on foot to Massachusetts Avenue, as visitors were caught in a bottleneck created by the new embassy's narrow doorway. It was "like the woman who bought shoes too small for her feet to look elegant," sniffed *Times-Herald* columnist Igor Cassini. "But you've got to suffer to be beautiful!"

The crush was exacerbated as hats and coats were tucked into dumbwaiters on both sides of the tiny foyer, using a system copied from the Hotel Savoy in London, to be dropped to a cloakroom below. (The *Washington Post* was unimpressed with these "robot hat-checkers, the very latest gadgets for ultra-modern living. . . . The guests were too fast, and the dumbwaiters were too slow.") In line, the German envoy bumped into the Australian minister, but no talk of the ongoing war was overheard. The chief of protocol, George Summerlin, was caught between the comers and the goers, Cassini reported, "and it required all his long experience of diplomatc ceremonials to get out of the place alive, but not without having crushed some innocent feet."

Inside, orchids by the hundreds from the Venezuelan jungles had been flown in for the affair. Cassini spotted the French ambassador, "who could not even raise his arm to arrange his mustache, due to the crowd." Dancing to Barnee's Orchestra, cork-popping, drinks of "whiskey and soda on tap" were had by many.

Ambassador Escalante described the $200,000 residence, designed by New York architect Chester A. Patterson, as "a house, not a palace." The building's wide expanse of windows outside, likened at the time to a pavilion at the previous year's New York World's Fair, was inside married to Venezuelan touches with pleasing effect. A solarium was added in 1965, and a covered swimming pool was built on the east side of the house in 1967.

At the time of the building's housewarming, *Washington Daily News* writer Evelyn Peyton Gordon described the 20-room concrete structure, covered in white stucco, as "semi-modern." The residence as well as the chancery annex on California Street—the first to be built by a Latin American nation in Washington—did not suggest Venezuela, and both buildings were certainly a departure from the ornate style favored along Embassy Row. The triangular lot, purchased from several owners, covers two-thirds of an acre.

The American legation in Caracas and the new Venezuelan diplomatic presence in Washington were elevated at this time to the

status of embassies, the latter moving from a 16th Street apartment.

The house features a huge salon, a downstairs game room, and a library paneled in Venezuelan mahogany, with carved scrolls symbolizing the nation's agriculture, literature, and justice. Flower gardens surround the building on three sides. The residence includes many paintings, such as Pedro Centano's *The Three Races,* which depicts three graceful nudes representing Venezuela's ethnic diversity. The ambassador's wife, Georgiana Gonzalez, admitted to a visitor in 1953 that the provocative painting draws considerable comment. "We found it tucked away in the cellar when we came here and immediately rehung it," she told the *Daily News.* "Most people enjoy it—except those who sit with their backs to the picture. One guest suggested [hanging] an opposite mirror; he had a stiff neck at the end of dinner because he turned constantly to join the comment!"

Centano also painted the striking panels of the nation's historical heroes, including Simon Bolívar and Guaicaipuro, a native South American who fought valiantly against the Spanish occupiers.

Venezuela has filled its ambassador's residence with classicist and abstract artwork — and some that is controversial.
Following pages: The unadorned, white stucco building departed from most of the city's richly wrought diplomatic buildings.

Further Reading

BOOKS

Applewhite, E. J. *Washington Itself.* New York: Alfred A. Knopf, 1961.

Cox, Warren J., Hugh Newell Jacobsen, Francis D. Lethbridge, and David R. Rosenthal. *A Guide to the Architecture of Washington, D.C.,* 2nd ed. New York: McGraw-Hill, 1974.

Eig, Emily Hotaling. "Kalorama: Two Centuries of Beautiful Views." In *Washington at Home,* Kathryn Schneider Smith, ed. Washington, D.C.: Windsor Publications, 1988.

Goode, James M. *Capital Losses: A Cultural History of Washington's Destroyed Buildings.* Washington, D.C.: Smithsonian Institution Press, 1979.

Goodwill Embassy Tour and Gala programs, 1947–91 (written in recent years by Allison Brown). Washington, D.C.: Davis Memorial Goodwill Industries.

Hammond, John Hays. *The Autobiography of John Hays Hammond,* 2 vols. New York: Farrar & Rinehard, 1935.

Highsmith, Carol, and Ted Landphair. *Pennsylvania Avenue: America's Main Street.* Washington, D.C.: American Institute of Architects Press, 1988.

Kreysa, Peter. *Diplomatic Dishes: A Cook's Tour of the Embassies.* Washington, D.C.: Maehlmann Press, 1989.

Kohler, Sue A., and Jeffrey R. Carson. *Sixteenth Street Architecture,* vols. 1 and 2. Washington, D.C.: Commission of Fine Arts, 1978.

Jennings, J. L., Jr., Sue A. Kohler, and Jeffrey R. Carson. *Massachusetts Avenue Architecture,* vols. 1 and 2. Washington, D.C.: Commission of Fine Arts, 1973, 1975.

McLean, Evalyn Walsh, with Boyden Sparkes. *Father Struck It Rich.* New York: Little, Brown, 1936.

Miller, Hope Ridings. Photographs by Charles Baptie. *Great Houses of Washington, D.C.* New York: C. N. Potter, 1969.

Miller, Hope Ridings. *Embassy Row: The Life & Times of Diplomatic Washington.* New York: Holt, Rinehart and Winston, 1969.

Mitchell, Henry. Photographs by Derry Moore. *Washington: Houses of the Capital.* New York: Viking Press, 1982.

Smith, A. Robert, and Eric Sevareid. *Washington: Magnificent Capital.* Garden City, N.Y.: Doubleday, 1965.

W.P.A. Guide to Washington, D.C. Federal Writers' Project of the Works Progress Administration for the District of Columbia. New York: Pantheon Books, 1942.

MAGAZINE ARTICLES, REPORTS, AND PAMPHLETS

Andrus, Patrick. "Sheridan-Kalorama Historic District: Evaluation of Potential National Significance" (report). Washington, D.C.: U.S. Department of the Interior, National Park Service, October 30, 1989.

"Comprehensive Plan for the National Capital." In "Foreign Missions and International Organizations" chapter and "Federal Elements" map supplement. Washington, D.C.: National Capital Planning Commission, 1978.

Conroy, Sarah Booth. "The Era of Elegant Embassies." *Washington Post Potomac* magazine, January 25, 1976.

"The Embassy of Venezuela." Report by the Embassy's Information Service. Washington, D.C., 1970.

Fawcett, Waldon. "Envoys at Washington." *The Cosmopolitan,* May 1901.

Forbes, Quinn. "The British Embassy." *The Illustrated American,* November 28, 1896.

"Foreign Missions and International Organizations: Real Property Manual." Washington, D.C.: U.S. Department of State, 1987.

"History of the Residence of the South African Ambassador in Washington, D.C." Undated publication of the embassy of the Republic of South Africa.

"India's Corner of Washington." *Washington Post Potomac* magazine, October 20, 1968.

"Indonesian Embassy: Nomination to the National Register of Historic Places." Washington, D.C.: U.S. Department of the Interior, National Park Service, 1989.

Laghi, Archibishop Pio. "The True Nature of Papal Diplomacy." *Origins,* May 3, 1984.

"Massachusetts Avenue Historical District: Nomination to the National Register of Historic Places." Washington, D.C.: U.S. Department of the Interior, National Park Service, 1989.

McLellan, Diana. "Perfect Pitch: With Charm, Intelligence, and a Very Good Resumé, Henry Catto Is the Man for the Job—Almost Any Job." *Washingtonian,* August 1991.

"National Capital Landmarks." Recommendation to the National Capital Planning Commission and the Commission of Fine Arts. Washington, D.C.: Joint Committee on Landmarks, November 8, 1964.

"Old English" (Garrett House). *House and Garden,* September 1937.

Radlovic, Monty. "Iron Curtain Diplomats in Washington." *The Diplomat,* November 1952.

Reese, Thomas J., S.J. "Diplomatic Relations with the Vatican." *America,* March 16, 1985.

Shalett, Sidney. "Washington's Diplomatic Whirl." *Better Homes & Gardens,* October 1958.

"Sheraton-Kalorama Historical District: Nomination to the National Register of Historic Places." Washington, D.C.: U.S. Department of the Interior, National Park Service, 1989.

Spatz, Frances, and William Engle. "Magnificent Mary." *The American Weekly,* February 27, 1949.

Tully, Andrew. "Kremlin, U.S.A." *Collier's,* August 20, 1954.

"U.S.-Soviet Agreement on Embassy Construction in Washington. Public Information Series, U.S. Department of State, Bureau of Public Affairs, May 19, 1987.

Wood, Junius. "The World Beats a Path to our Doorstep." *Nation's Business,* August 1945.

EMBASSIES OF WASHINGTON WAS DESIGNED BY Rebecca S. Neimark of Meadows & Wiser, Washington, D.C. The text was set in Cochin, a typeface designed by Deberney & Peignot in 1910 as part of the revival of Renaissance-style typefaces in the early 20th century. The italic and display type was set in Bernhard, a face designed by Lucian Bernhard in 1937. The book was produced using Quark Xpress and Adobe Illustrator software on an Apple Macintosh computer. Page mechanicals were output by General Typographers, Inc., of Washington, D.C., and the book was printed through Palace Press, of Singapore.